The Restored Nurse

Matthew Norman, MSN, RN

Contents

Chapter One

Introduction

"I JUST WANT TO LOVE BEING A NURSE AGAIN!"

This was the exact sentence I screamed to God, as I stood in the woods, tears streaming down my face. I had been a nurse for nearly 20 years. For most of that time, I loved what I did. At that moment, I was seriously considering leaving nursing entirely. I didn't want to, but I didn't think there was any way that I could be happy in nursing. I didn't know it at the time, but this was the beginning of a journey that would help me restore my life in ways I didn't think possible. I'm not saying that nursing, or my life, are not without their problems, but I will say that the lessons I've learned on this journey have made my life so much better than I could have anticipated.

Nursing is hard.

Ok, this is hardly a secret. Anyone in nursing for even a short time knows this and even most people outside of it. We are understaffed, underpaid, and most definitely underappreciated. There was a time, during the height of the COVID pandemic, when the public and the institutions we work for hailed us as heroes. Just a short time later they both had turned against us, at least it felt that way. In some cases the institutions that we had dedicated our lives to even went so far as to see nurses prosecuted while covering up their own involvement in situations.

Nurses are struggling.

I know, because I was one of them. Like so many nurses, I found myself struggling and seriously considering leaving nursing entirely. I was able to work through that and rediscover the love for nursing that had been beaten out of me.

Now, I'm not saying that I am where I want to be, but I have become determined to learn what it means to take better care of ME. This has meant changing a lot of things in my life. I still have a long way to go, but I'm getting a little better each day. For years I've seen the nurses around me struggling as well. Many of them have different struggles that I do and different changes to make. Still, I think that all nurses can learn from the areas of my life where I have taken good care of myself, as well as learning from the lessons I'm learning as I travel on my journey.

Hi. My name is Matt Norman. I'm a nurse on a journey to learn what it means to take better care of myself and on a mission to bring as many nurses with me as possible.

I've been a nurse since 2000 and in healthcare even longer than that. For many of those years, I've also been a fully ordained pastor, working in a variety of roles within the church and even pastoring a church for a bit. Throughout my career, I've always kinda felt like my roles as pastor and nurse were two completely different things. Sure, I often ministered to people while serving in my nursing role and even saw that as a great opportunity to minister to people in their most difficult and lowest moments. Still, I felt like these two roles never really, fully crossed. I see this book and the work I'm doing through Restoring Nurses, as a true combination of these previously separate parts of my life.

A quick word about faith

As I mentioned above, I am a Christian and pastor. My faith is part of everything I do. Naturally, this makes it part of this journey to take better care of myself. As a Christian, I believe that there is wisdom in the Bible that applies to our lives, even these many years later. Throughout this book, I will be sharing a combination of biblical wisdom as well as lessons I've learned along my journey.

Does that mean this book is only for Christians? No.

I truly believe that the things I share in this book can be applied to anyone's life.

So, why do I share this word about my faith? Let's just call it transparency. I want people to know where I'm coming from. I know that many have negative opinions on Christianity and Christians. If that's you, I'm truly sorry for what you have experienced that led to those feelings. I just ask that you enter this book with an open mind.

The Restored Nurse, **What does that mean?**

I'm a huge car guy. I love pretty much anything with wheels. Sure I have my favorites, but if it has wheels I'm probably into it. I love watching these shows where auto restoration experts take some beat-up old car and bring it back to life. In many cases, the end result is better than the original. They start with what many would consider junk and end up with a car that has been RESTORED.

Merriam-Webster defines restore as, "to bring back to or put back into former or original state. To renew." In a physical sense, we are not going to be able to bring ourselves back to our original state, especially if you've been a nurse for a couple of decades or more like I have. However, I do believe that we can improve our health and get our bodies to a state of function that is much closer to when we started than many of us might think. I also believe that we can build some aspects of our lives into something BETTER than when we first became nurses.

In the Bible the Hebrew word that is translated as renew is *chadash*. This word is often used to refer to the restoration or refurbishment of a building. However, it is used in other places to refer to the renewal of our spirit, strength, or even our youth. I love this because that is exactly my goal with my journey and my goal for the nurses I'm working to help.

Most nurses start their careers with a passion for the job or for caring for others. Yet, many have had that passion stripped from them, or have seen it slowly erode over time. Many nurses can relate to the beat-up old car that enters the restoration shop. Many think that the passion and energy they had early in their career is gone forever. Even worse, some think that even finding joy in their life outside of nursing is impossible.

I, respectfully, disagree!

Just like the car I mentioned above, I believe that nurses can not only regain the passion they once had but can become better than they were in the beginning. My mission is to do just that, to RESTORE nurses into healthier, happier versions of themselves. In other words, to help nurses live a restored life.

What is a Restored Life?

Going back to the car analogy I used earlier let's try to relate to that car. Imagine you're on a trip with that restoration expert. You're checking out a rumor of a classic sports car under a blanket and a few decades of dust in a nearby barn. You travel to the property and meet the owner who shows you to the barn. Your heart rate elevates as the doors open and you see a car covered in a blanket. Even through the blanket, you can see the sexy curves that scream Corvette. The blanket is removed and your heart skips a beat. Hidden and ignored in this dirty barn is a 1967 Corvette Stingray, my all-time favorite car.

That car started life sexy, high-powered, and beautiful, just like you. Now it sits covered in many years of dust, dirt, and some things I'd rather not talk about. The car that was once tearing up the streets now can't even exit this barn under its own power. Somewhere along the line, this amazing car got discarded. Somebody stopped caring about it, or for it. It got ignored, forgotten, and, eventually broke down.

I think many of us can see a similar story in our careers as nurses. Nobody seems to care about us, nobody is caring for us, and we feel ignored, forgotten, and broken down.

As you get the car back to your shop, you start assessing all the things that are wrong with it, making a list of everything that needs to be fixed, rebuilt, or replaced. You break it down into systems like the engine, transmission, brakes, exterior, interior, etc. Then, little by little you start to address all of the issues and, over time, the car begins to take back its former glory. It takes time and hard work, but the results are worth it. By the time you're done, the car is not only back to how it once looked, but some aspects of it are better than when it was new.

A restored life is kinda like that. You first have to determine where you are starting. I've built an assessment for that, which I'll put in the appendix of this book. From there you make a list of everything that needs to be addressed and start working on it. I've broken down that list of "systems" into what I call the Six Pillars of the Restored Life. I'll talk more about those in a little bit.

When all of these areas have been returned to health, then you are living a "restored" life. Just like rebuilding that car, this process is going to take time and hard work, but the results will be worth it. The good news is that you will experience results throughout the process.

Before we move on, let me say one more thing about that classic car and how it relates to my journey and yours. When the restoration is complete, the work on that car is not done. If we never give the car any more attention, then it will slowly move back into the condition it was in when we found it. The same goes for us. If we achieve what we would consider a restored life, and start to neglect any of the 6 Pillars, then we will find that that area slowly moves back to where we came from. I, for one, am not interested in going back to where I have come from.

Ok, how did we get here?

Nurses are some of the best people you'll ever meet. In the 20-plus years I've been a nurse, I have seen so many beautiful moments between nurses and their patients and between nurses and other healthcare workers. Nurses constantly give of themselves, often with little thought to their own well-being.

Seldom will you see a more giving person than a nurse. We will pour out of ourselves until we have nothing left. Sadly, the same nurse who is so committed to caring for their patients and families often does little to care for themselves. Many feel guilty for even considering taking time to do this.

I once asked a bunch of nurses what the biggest barriers were between them and proper self-care. The answers included things like money, time, and a lack of knowledge, among other things. One that came up over and over again was guilt. These people who have dedicated their lives to caring for people both at work and in their day-to-day lives, often don't think that they are worthy of care.

How can these people who give so much, think themselves so undeserving?

I think this starts as early as nursing school. I can still remember the orientation for my nursing program, 25 or more years ago. The director got up in front of the group and told us to say goodbye to our friends and family for the next two years. What she was saying, and what she truly believed, was that we were not going to have time for anything except nursing school. While she specifically mentioned relationships, it later became evident that this meant even things like our mental and physical health as well. This experience is common among many nurses and even today persists. A nursing friend once told me about being told that she was a nurse now and didn't have time for a mental illness. With stories like these, is it any wonder nurses struggle to care for themselves?

While the, "say goodbye to the people you care about" speech was very overt, some of our problems are more covert. They are hidden among the things that we are taught. You see, from day one something that is pounded into us in nursing school is that we are to be advocates for our patients. This message continues throughout our career. This is a good message. We absolutely MUST advocate for our patients. There will be times when we are the only people advocating for them.

But, who advocates for us?

These days many people are advocating for nursing as a profession. However, there is often no one advocating for the individual nurse. There is seldom anyone advocating for the physical, mental, spiritual, relational, or financial health of the nurse. Let's not even talk about work health. Not only are our employers not advocating for our work health, but they are often the reason we struggle with it and even try to make us feel guilty if we seek a healthier work life.

If we, as nurses, refuse to advocate for ourselves, we are left with no one advocating for us.

Watering cans, not hoses

When I think of this, I often think of a watering can. I am by no means a gardener, but let's say that I was. Suppose I grab my trusty watering can and go out to water my plants. One by one I pour out of my watering can and give each plant what it needs. As I give to each plant, my watering can becomes more and more empty. At some point, I will have to refill my watering can if I am going to continue watering my plants. Failure to do this will cause the remainder of my plants to suffer.

We are much like that watering can. We go through life pouring out of ourselves and into other people. One by one we give the people around us what they need and each time we do, our stores become less and less. At some point, we have to take time to refill ourselves or we will run out.

Nurses tend to think of themselves more as hoses. You see, instead of a watering can, I could drag the entire hose out into my garden. With that hose, I have a virtually limitless supply of water. No matter how much I water my plants that hose is unlikely to run out. We, however, do not have an endless supply. We are not water hoses, we are more like watering cans. If we don't take time to refill, we WILL run out and it WILL affect the way we care for the people around us. The very people we are so passionate about caring for will suffer because we refuse to care for ourselves.

Guilt over resentment

Dr. John Delony is a popular podcaster and personality. I listen to every episode he puts out. On his show, he takes calls and helps people work through their mental health, relationships, and other issues. One thing he often tells people is to choose guilt over resentment. What he's saying is that we often do things we don't want to do, because we will feel guilty if we don't do them. Over time, doing these things has a real likelihood of making us resent the things we are doing or the people we do them for. He says it's better to feel guilty about not going to a family event, or whatever it is than to come to resent those people because you went against your values or desires.

This is such a problem in nursing. As I mentioned earlier, guilt is one of the main reasons nurses give for not caring for themselves. That guilt leads us not to care for ourselves and, over time, often turns into resentment for nursing, patients, employers, or the other people who require our care. It is very common for nurses to work late, pick up extra shifts, or come in when called because they feel guilty saying no. This, too, can turn into resentment, over time.

In the long run, a short time of feeling guilty is better than years of resentment.

What, then, is self-care

If you asked 10 people what self-care was, you'd get at least 7-8 different answers. Some of these answers would likely include things like meals out, or weekends away. Some would include something to do with alcohol. Others might talk about pampering with things like manicures, pedicures, or purchases made for themselves. While these are not bad things, I would argue that they are incomplete, in the least.

Other folks might talk about exercise and eating right. This is good, but still incomplete. I've known nurses who were in great physical shape, but lived on the very verge of a breakdown... or worse. I've known others who had great mental health, but their families were falling apart. At its most basic, self-care is simply taking care of yourself. The struggle is defining exactly what that looks like in our lives.

So, if it's not about dinner out with family or friends, trips to the beach, or pampering ourselves, what is it all about?

As I have worked to learn what this means for me. I've broken self-care into six domains:

1. Work Health

2. Physical health

3. Mental health

4. Spiritual health

5. Relational health

6. Financial health

I am convinced that all of these are connected. They can work together to help us build a restored life, or they can work together to bring us down. We can excel in one of these and fail in another and the end result will be a failure to build the restored life you so badly want... and deserve.

Consider this:

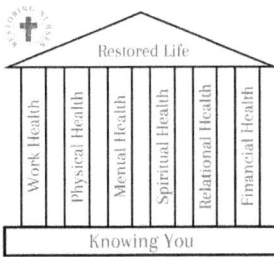

The restored life is the roof of this building.

Throughout the remainder of this book, I'm going to talk about each of these six pillars. In each chapter, I'll start by helping you evaluate where you are with that specific pillar. Not so much measuring your status or performance in it, but rather looking at your habits as it relates to each pillar. I believe that our lives, as they are today, are mostly a result of the habits that have been in our lives up to this point. Certainly, there are circumstances and other things that affect where we are in life, but most of it is a result of the habits that have brought us here. For each pillar, we will evaluate your current habits to see what they can tell you about where you are starting.

Is self-care selfish?

When I polled nurses about their barriers to self-care one sentiment that came up many times was that they felt that taking care of themselves was selfish. Some even said that people in their lives had gone so far as to say as much. Outside of that poll, I've heard many people express that self-care felt selfish. So, is it?

Ephesians 5:29 says, "For no one ever hates his own flesh but provides and cares for it, just as Christ does for the church since we are members of His body."

This verse is actually talking about marriage. Still, there are a couple of things we can take from this as it relates to self-care. First, it shows that to not "provide for and care for" our flesh is equal to hating it. While many of us might feel that self-care is selfish, would any of us go so far as to say that we hate our very flesh? Ok, full transparency, there have been times when I looked in the mirror and hated the shape I've allowed my body to get in. Still, even with that, I wouldn't say that I hate my body itself, just the condition I've allowed it to get into.

This verse goes on to say that the person mentioned provides for and cares for his own body as Christ cares for the church. Wow, I'm not sure I can think of any better illustration of caring than that of Jesus caring for His church. As I read this I can't help but think that not only is self-care not selfish, it is a good thing.

Let's look at another verse.

Matthew chapter 22 Jesus is asked, "Which command in the law is the greatest?" Jesus responds with "Love the Lord your God with all your heart, with all your soul, and with all your strength." Here Jesus is quoting a passage known as the Shema, found in Deuteronomy 6:5. While He was not asked about the second greatest command, He goes on to offer one, "The second is like it: Love your neighbors as yourself." Keeping in mind that these are the very words of Jesus, let's consider this.

To "love your neighbor as yourself" is not a call to self-love. Still, it does assume that loving and caring for yourself is happening. After all, if you are not caring and loving yourself, then you can not "love your neighbor as yourself."

Ok, but what does that MEAN?

As a nurse, you have committed yourself to helping people care for their physical health. If you are to love your neighbor in that way, you should do the same for yourself. Maybe you are a psychiatric nurse and have, therefore, committed yourself to caring for the mental health of others. Just like with physical health, if you are going to love your neighbor by caring for their mental health, you must also care for yourself by caring for your own. This same concept could be applied to all six of the pillars. We've covered physical and mental health, but it applies just as much to work health, spiritual health, relational health, and financial health.

Ok, but does this answer the question, "Is self-care selfish?" Well, I would argue that Jesus makes it clear that self-care is something we should be doing. So, we have to ask, "Would Jesus tell us to do it if it was selfish?" I certainly don't think so.

So, no, self-care is not selfish.

A journey, not a destination

This first part gives us a starting point. This whole life restoration thing is not a destination, but a journey. Setting out on any journey requires that you first know where you are starting from. Once, that has been established, we can determine our destination. These two points work together to help us form a plan for getting from one to the other.

I love road trips. There is something about the freedom of starting whenever you want, stopping wherever you want, and doing what you want along the way. I've been on a number of epic road trips in my life. While each of them had a destination and these destinations were memorable, the stories I tell from these trips are often more about things that happened along the way.

Like the time I almost died in a 1987 IROC Camaro driving through the Smokey Mountains. Or how the muffler of that very same Camaro fell off while we were driving through the mountains and we used my buddy's shoestring to hold it up. Or the time I missed my turn going to Cocoa Beach with my girlfriend, now wife, and ended up in Daytona Beach instead. Or how we decided to jump on the interstate and drive down to Cocoa Beach because that's where we wanted to be... like there was something wrong with Daytona Beach. I could go on. As I think about this, I can think of more stories about the journey of my different road trips than about the destinations themselves.

You see, a road trip is at least as much about the journey as it is about the destination. The journey may be even MORE important than the destination. I wouldn't go so far as to say that the journey toward a restored life is more important than the restored life itself, but we tend to get so focused on the destination that we fail to enjoy the journey or celebrate the victories that we experience along the way.

Before going into the next section, move over to *The Restored Nurse Companion Workbook*, page 32, and complete the exercise you find there. The workbook includes an entire chapter on mindset that I wrote after writing this book, specifically for the workbook. It also includes new exercises that are no included in this book.

How to use this book

By now, you may be eager to dive into the content, hungry to get into the meat of what it means to build and live a restored life. Truth is I'm eager for you to get into it as well. However, before we do that I thought I'd share a few thoughts about how to use this book.

Some of you may want to read cover to cover. This is a great option. Ignoring any of these six pillars will greatly limit the potential of the restored life you are trying to build. Each of these crosses over others. The only way to fully build and live a restored life is to make sure that all of these things are taken care of, and growing. So, reading all of the chapters through is a great option.

Others, however, are going to want to give more attention to a given pillar, while still working on the others. Maybe you recognize that one of these pillars requires much more work and you want to get right on that. If that's you, I would encourage you to read Chapter 2. This chapter is going to help you set the foundations on which all of the pillars are built. Once you've done that, feel free to jump ahead to whichever pillar you think needs the most attention.

Still, others may have no idea where they would start. If this is you, then I would encourage you to read chapter two, and then take my Restored Life Assessment for Nurses. You can find this at restorin gnurses.com/assessment. This assessment is going to help you define where you are at in each of the six pillars. This can give you an idea of where to start.

Ok, now let's get into it.

Desired Outcomes, Actional Goals., and Measures of Success

One more thing before we move on to chapter 2

DESIRED OUTCOMES

A multitude of books have been written on good goal setting. There is great content in many of them... but I think they are wrong. Ok, I'm not really saying that they are completely wrong. I just think that most of us focus on the wrong things when we do goal-setting.

Consider this; let's say that you set a goal to that you want to lose weight. That's a great goal, but it's weak. To make it a little stronger, you put a number to it. You want to lose 50 pounds. This is better, but still not quite there. Going a step further, you say that you want to lose 50 pounds over the next six months. NOW you have a good goal... at least according to most folks.

I don't agree... at least not completely.

You see, goals such as this focus on the results, while ignoring the actions and behaviors that will work to get us there. The reality is that you cannot MAKE yourself lose weight. You can, however, make yourself do the actions and behaviors that will cause you to lose weight.

For this reason, we are not going to talk about goals. Instead, we are going to talk about DESIRED OUTCOMES.

Going back to the above goal-setting example, instead of saying that your goal is to lose 50 pounds, we are going to call that your DESIRED OUTCOME. I know that this sounds like I'm making a big deal out of nothing, but stick with me it will make more sense.

Conventional goal setting focuses not only on the results, but it tends to be too narrow, in my opinion. You may set a goal to lose 50 pounds, and that's a good thing, but how do you want your life to change as a result of the changes you are making?

A couple of years ago I had the honor of being the announcer for the home football games at my alma mater high school. This meant walking up the rather high bleacher steps at the football stadium to get up to the press box. Let me tell you, the first time I did it, I thought I was going to DIE by the time I got to the top. My heart rate had jumped to 160 and I was sucking wind as if I had just run some sort of sprint. The bleachers were tall, but they were not THAT tall. So, one of my desired outcomes became to be able to walk up those bleachers without feeling like I was going to die.

About five weeks ago, as of the writing of this, our first grandchild was born. As we found out that he was coming, one of my desired outcomes became to be able to get on the floor or run around in the yard and play with him when he got a little older.

Here's another one. Our daughter will soon turn 16. Someday she will find a man who wants to spend the rest of his life with her. I had the honor a couple years ago to perform our son's wedding. I want to be around to walk my daughter down the aisle and then to perform her ceremony. The man I have been, one who didn't take care of his body, was leading me to the very real potential of not being around for that.

While losing 50 pounds is a great thing to strive for, you can see how these other desired outcomes are much more personal. These mean a lot more to me than simply a number of a scale, or even the size of clothes that I wear.

Hopefully, you get what I mean by "desired outcomes". Losing 50 pounds is a great desired outcome. However, as we work through each pillar in the coming sections, I want you to think way deeper than this. Great desired outcomes include what you want your life to look like in the future, at how you want your life to FEEL, and how YOU want to feel.

ACTIONABLE GOALS

Wait I thought we had decided we weren't going to talk about goals. Well, that is partially true. What I actually said was that we were going to look at goals a little differently. What most people would call goals, we are not calling Desired Outcomes. So, what do I mean by ACTIONABLE GOALS.

Well, most people's goals focus on the outcome they want, as we've already discussed. Where this fails is that it gives no consideration for the actions and behaviors that will move us toward our desired outcomes. Actionable Goals are the input we put in so that we have the outcome we desire.

If we are honest, we cannot MAKE ourselves lose weight. Stay with me, I know that sounds crazy. What we CAN do is take steps that will move us towards losing weight. THIS is what we can control.

For instance, let say I spent all of my time thinking about how much I wanted to lose weight, but I never changed anything about my nutrition or activity levels. The result will not be lost weight. However, if I make adjustments to my nutrition or activity level that are consistent with weight loss, then I will likely lose weight.

Actional goals are the things we can control. Ok, let's consider some of the desired outcomes I mentioned earlier.

- Lost 50 pounds: For this one, I might set an actionable goal of tracking my calories and staying within my calorie goals at least 6 of 7 days. Or, I might set a weekly calorie budget

with an actionable goal of tracking my calories every day and
staying within that budget.

- Climb the bleachers without feeling like I'm going to die: To
  move myself towards this desired outcome, I might set a goal
  to walk a certain distance 5-6 days per week.

- To be able to get on the floor and play with my grandson: Here I might set a goal of doing resistance training 3-4
  days per week in order to build and maintain my muscular
  strength and bone density.

In each of these, you can see that the goals are ACTIONS that I
control. These focus on the INPUT that will move me towards the
OUTCOME that I want.

Another note on actionable goals; these can start small and grow
as you progress. So, the walking goal may start with just 3-4 days and
grow from there. It might start as a goal of walking for 30 minutes,
and grow from there. As I progress, I can continue to extend the goal
so that it grows with me.

MEASURES OF SUCCESS

The purpose of The Restored Nurse, this workbook, and my Restored Life workshops is to help you build the life you want to live,
a RESTORED LIFE. With our desired outcomes we paint a picture
of what that life looks and feels like, but how do we know that our
actionable goals are actually moving us towards those outcomes? This
is where measures of success come in.

Measures of success identify how we are going to gauge our
success, not just in the end, but as we progress through the process. If

a measure of success shows, over time, that you are not moving toward your desired outcome, then you need to go back and take another look at your actionable goals and consider what you need to adjust to get you moving in that direction.

Consider the previously discussed desired outcomes:

- Lost 50 pounds: This one's easy. The measure of success would be periodic weigh-ins. While weight is not the only measure of improved health, fitness, or the effectiveness of our actionable goals, if we have a specific goal of losing 50 pounds, then weighing ourselves from time to time will tell us if what we are doing is working.

- Climb the bleachers without feeling like I'm going to die: Here I might find some stairs to climb. To make this as good as possible, I'd try to go to the same staircase and use measurements such as time, number of stairs, and heart rate to be able to track my improvement.

- To be able to get on the floor and play with my grandson: This is another easy one. To answer the question if I'm becoming better able to get on the floor and play with my grandson, I could simply get on the floor. How easy is it for me to get back up? Maybe I'll play with my dog while I'm down there. Do I feel unusually short of breath while I'm doing this? Do I feel better than I used to?

QUICK RECAP

- **Desired outcomes**: These paint a picture of what the life you are building will look and feel like.

- **Actionable goals**: Desired outcomes tell us where we are going. Actionable goals tell us how we are going to get there. These are the actions and behaviors that we are going to put into place in order to move us toward those desired outcomes.

- **Measures of success**: This is how we will determine if our actionable goals are working. These help us to determine when we have achieved the life we are working to build, but also help us to track our progress along the way.

Ok, now you have my permission to move on to chapter 2.

Chapter Two

Who are you

"If I'm not a nurse, who am I?"

As I cried out to God this was the question that I faced. I swore I'd never allow myself to be identified by a job. Yet, here I was feeling a sense of loss at the very idea of leaving nursing. It made me feel empty. I truly didn't know who I'd be if I was no longer a nurse. Worse than that, I felt as if I would have no worth. Sure, I still had personal worth but what could I offer an employer when all I had ever known was nursing? Nearly two decades in the field had given me knowledge and experience that was of great value... so long as I continued to be a nurse. If I wasn't a nurse, it felt as if all that experience and knowledge were worthless.

All the other pieces of who I am didn't matter. I was looking at losing the part of me that was a nurse and it hurt. Still, I'm glad it happened. You see, it was the beginning of me taking back my identity. No longer would I be so completely consumed by my work that it would overtake my identity. The journey has helped me to connect with the parts of me that are far more important and made me a better husband, father, friend, and more.

Who am I?

Throughout my childhood and adolescence, I saw people around me who seemed consumed with the job they did. The job seemed so important to them that it would cause them to make decisions that might have been good for the job but were bad for other aspects of their lives. It was as if a major part of their identity was wrapped up in the job and the work. I saw the negative effects this had on their families and swore I would never be like that.

As I entered college and decided I was going to become a nurse, I swore that I would not let it consume me. I would never let the job define who I was. Somewhere along the line, I found that I had drifted away from that conviction. Somehow nurse had become not simply what I did, but who I was. Nurse is absolutely PART of who I am, as it should be. However, I found it had become such a part of who I was that it was beginning to affect other aspects of my life.

It was through the process of self-exploration that I discuss in this chapter that I was able to get back to the things that truly mattered most to me. I still love being a nurse and it is still an important part of who I am, I am just determined not to let it become such a big part of who I am that the things and people in my life that matter more begin to suffer.

Foundations

Up to this point, you've heard me talk about the six pillars of a restored life. I like to think of the six pillars as columns that hold up a roof. That roof is the restored life. Without the six pillars, the roof crumbles and falls. In the same way, the pillars need something solid to stand on, or they will fall, bringing the roof down with them.

Knowing who you are is the foundation upon which we will build and support our six pillars.

About now you may be thinking I've lost my mind. You might be asking yourself, "How does knowing who I am support or even relate to these other things." Stick with me and I'll explain.

I said that the question of who we are, beyond our name, is something most of us have never considered. As I've traveled on my restoration journey, I've given quite a bit of thought to this. Early in my career, I made a decision that I never wanted to allow my job to become my identity. Certainly, the job we do is an important part of who we are, but I never wanted it to consume too large a part of me. Somewhere along the way, the very thing I didn't want to happen, happened. I suddenly found myself considering leaving nursing and struggling with who I would be if I were no longer working as a nurse. Nursing had become such a part of me that I felt I'd be lost if I was no longer doing it.

At this time I began a process of diving deep to determine who I was and, as a result, what it was that mattered most to me. More about that later, but now let's talk a bit more about foundations.

In Luke 6:47-49 Jesus talks about two men building houses. One He tells us dug deep to find a firm foundation and build his house on that. The other did not dig deep and built his house on the sand. A flood came and both houses were tested.

For the first man, we are told that "...the river crashed against that house and it couldn't shake it, because it was well built" This house was built on a firm foundation. The second man built his house on the ground without a foundation and, "...the river crashed against it, and immediately it collapsed. And the destruction of that house was great."

When we don't have firm foundations upon which our lives are built or are being built, we are like the man who build his house on the ground, without a foundation. The storms of life will come and crash against us and we will crumble. These storms come in the form of a thousand priorities, requests, and demands on our time and energy. With a firm foundation, of who you are and what is important to you, you can face these storms, see how they line up with your values, and ward off the ones that don't. Without this foundation, when the storm comes, you will crumble and give in to the priorities of others, and so many requests and demands, even if they don't line up with the life you want to build.

This river will come and it will beat against our "home". If we are not prepared for it, then we will give in to these many influences. Before we know it the life we were trying to live has come crashing down, just like the house built on the ground, without a foundation.

One final thing about foundations. It can be easy to skip over something that passage tells us about foundations. Sure, we easily recognize that it is important. However, if we don't look closely we can miss what might be even more important. The first man built his house on a foundation and it survived the flood. But, to get to that foundation he had to dig deep. This is the piece we might miss. Building your restored life on a foundation is going to require that you dig deep. For the remainder of this chapter, I'm going to help you take a deep look into who you are and what matters most. Then I'm going to help you build boundaries based on those things.

Who are you?

Suppose that you and I met at a local coffee shop. You ask me who I am. On the surface, this seems like a pretty simple question. My automatic answer would likely be that I am Matt Norman. This is a perfectly reasonable answer. It's who I have been for my entire life. Suppose that you then leaned in and said, "Ok, but who is Matt Norman?"

That is a much more complicated question.

For most of us, this is a question we have likely never considered. This question requires that we dig deeper than most of us ever have or are comfortable doing. I would argue, however, that this is crucial to building and living a restored life. You see, it is out of this second question that we are able to clarify the things that matter most to us. When we have taken the time to identify these things, then we can begin to build a life around those pieces of who we are. Most of us seldom, if ever actually think about this. The unfortunate result of this is that different areas of our lives begin to choose, for themselves, their place in our lives.

We talked about foundations earlier. I believe that who you say you are is foundational to the life you want to build. A high view of yourself helps you build a better life. Likewise, a low view of yourself will often lead you to build a life that is not as fulfilling or healthy. At the very least, this low view will work to slow down your progress.

Who does God say you are?

We'll talk a bit more about who you are and how you can do the deep work needed to connect with that later. Before we do, I wanted to take a look at Who God, through the Bible, says you are.

THE RESTORED NURSE 27

The phrase, "Who am I", is seen throughout the Bible. In Exodus 3:11, Moses says it as an expression of doubt in his worth or ability to do what God was calling him to do. As we read further we read where God says that HE would empower Moses to do what he was being called to. Man, imagine God saying that HE was going to give you what you needed to do the things He has called you to do. The good news is that God makes that exact promise through His word. Philippians 1:6 says, "I am sure of this, that He who started a good work in you will carry it on to completion..." God has started a good work in you and He has promised to see it to completion. Allow that to encourage you to push forward in building your restored life. In another section, David, used this very same phrase, "Who am I," to express humility. As important as it is to let the story of Moses encourage us, let's also remember the humility of David.

Ok, so who does God say you are?

Who better to say who you are than the one who created you? Here are a just few examples of verses showing who God says you are:

- "... remarkably and wonderfully made..." Psalm 139:14

- "... no longer slaves, but a son (or daughter) and if a son (or daughter) then an heir through God." Galatians 4:7

- Children of God. John 1:12

- A new creation. 2 Corinthians 5:17

- Friends of Jesus. John 15:15

This is just a small sample of who God says you are. The question then becomes, who do YOU say you are?

Who do you say you are?

We talked earlier about the question of who you are being more than simply your name. This is certainly part of who you are, but I would argue that it fails to say much about you. Heck, your name is likely not even something you chose. It was likely given to you by your parents or perhaps, if you're a married woman, you might have taken your husband's last name. Even in that case, you chose him, but that doesn't necessarily mean you chose the name.

So, who are you? Like beyond your name, as we discussed earlier. Who are you?

As I mentioned, this is something I've given some thought to. For me, the result was a list that includes things such as:

- Christian, Husband, Father, Friend, Pastor, Nurse, Mentor, Maker, Musician, And more

Why does this list matter? I believe that building that firm foundation we've been talking about starts with this.

EXERCISE 2

Now it's time to do some work. Get a blank sheet of paper or a notebook. It can be lined, or blank, whatever works for you. Take a few minutes and think of every word you can come up with that describes a piece of who you are. Consider my list as a place to start. As you do this, keep in mind that the list I shared here is far from complete. Your list doesn't have to be huge, but the goal is to make sure to include as many of these labels as you can come up with. At this time, don't worry about putting it in any kind of order. Just put down as many as come to mind.

Once you've taken some time to make your initial list, set it aside. Then throughout the next day, continue to think about all the words that describe part of who you are. When you think of another one, add it to your list. You may want to continue this process for the next several days. Once you feel like your list is more or less complete, come back to this book and move on to the next part.

> You can complete this exercise on page 34 in *The Restored Nurse Companion Workbook*

What matters most?

If I were to ask you, "What are the most important things in your life," how would you answer? Would it be your kids? Maybe your spouse? Maybe your relationship with Jesus? Maybe even your job, profession, or your patients? The reality is that most of us have probably never actually given this much thought. Sure, if I asked you this question, you could come up with a quick answer, but is this something you have truly taken time to think about?

In Matthew 6:21 Jesus says, "...for where your treasure is, your heart will be also..." In this passage, Jesus is specifically talking about not focusing so much on earthly things that we miss heavenly or eternal things. Still, there is more that we can learn from this verse. First, to Jesus' point, if we are not careful, we can allow things that are of less importance to distract us from things that really matter. The second lesson is that we can tell what matters to a person by how they spend their money. I've often heard it said like this, "If you want to know what a person really cares about, look at their bank account."

We each have limited resources to give to the many different pieces of who we are. How we spend these resources can tell us a lot about what we truly value. I love Dave Ramsey. I know he's not everyone's cup of tea, but I love to listen to his podcast and think that most of the things he says are really quite good. When he talks about budgeting he says that a budget is you telling your money what to do. Without it, he explains, your money just kinda does what it wants to. In my experience what my money seems to want to do is disappear.

I think there are three primary resources we have that we can "spend" on the many different pieces of ourselves. These include time, energy, and money. We read where Jesus said that we can tell a lot about a person by how they spend their money. I would argue that the same is true for the things we give our time and energy to. Even as you can tell what matters to a person by checking their bank account, you can also tell a lot by checking their calendar.

So, what matters most in your life?

If we looked at your bank account would it reflect that? What about your calendar? What would it say about the things that matter most? Let's do some more work.

EXERCISE 3

By now you should have a list of words that describe part of who you are. In that exercise, we didn't worry about putting them in order. The goal was simply to compile the list. Now, we are going to put them in order.

So, now look back at the list you made. Read over it carefully. Start putting numbers next to them. Look for the one that is MOST important and put a "1" next to it. Now, number 2 and so forth. If you have a lengthy list, I wouldn't worry about trying to number the entire list. Focus on finding the top 5-8.

Once you've completed this, take a blank piece of paper, or turn to a fresh sheet in your notebook, and write those items in order on this sheet. When that's done, set it aside and walk away from it. Try not to think about it for a bit. Seriously. I want you not to think about this list for a while. Maybe even a day or two. When you're ready, go back and look at the list again. Does it still feel right? Are they in the correct order? Is there anything on the list that doesn't feel right? Is anything missing? Come back to your list a few times until it feels right. When it does, continue in the book.

> *The Restored Nurse Companion Workbook*, page 36.

Boundaries

By now you've made a list of words that describe pieces of who you are. You've taken that list and placed it in order of importance. The result is a list of the top 5-10 parts of who you are. For me, the top three include Christian, husband, and father. Yours may look quite different than mine and that's ok. What we now have to look at is how we protect those things that we've now said are most important to us. This is where boundaries come into play.

So, what are boundaries? What comes to mind for you when you hear this word? In his book *Boundaries,* Dr. Henry Cloud equates boundaries in our lives with the boundaries around our homes. With my home, there is a clear boundary of where my property begins. You can go down to the county and get official records showing where that boundary lies. As a homeowner, I get to decide what goes on within that boundary, so long as it doesn't negatively affect others. Within that boundary is my home. This represents yet another boundary. Inside my home there is a higher level of control and, as a result, greater expectations.

Consider this. If someone wants to park in the street in front of my house every day, I might find it annoying but the street is outside the boundary of my property and there isn't much I can do about it. If that same person parked in my driveway, they are now within the boundary of my property and I can have their car towed. Suppose that same person then tried to break into my home or they got into my home and tried to harm my family. There I could take even more extreme action. You see, with each additional boundary, my authority and level of control increases.

What does this have to do with building a restored life?

Just as the boundaries of my home define where my control and authority lie, so do boundaries in our lives. In my experience, this is something that many nurses struggle with. For that matter, I think most people in general struggle with setting healthy boundaries. A boundary can be as simple as how you will allow people to talk to you. Yes, that's right, even as a nurse, you don't have to let people talk to you disrespectfully. A boundary may be the number of hours you're willing to work in a week or life events that you are unwilling to miss.

How can boundaries help you protect the things you've identified as most important in your life? To help with that, let me tell you about Alice. Alice is a completely made-up person, but I think that her story is one that many of us can relate to.

Alice is a nurse working in a local hospital. She's been a nurse for about 4 years. She loves the work of being a nurse. She loves caring for people, but some of the other parts of the job are starting to weigh on her. Alice is married to Tom, Sr. They have two kids; Tommy, 14, and Sarah, 8. Tommy plays baseball and Sara is a dancer. Alice tries to encourage both of her kids in these pursuits, but her job often means that she can't be there for all their stuff.

On a Friday night, Alice is sitting in the living room watching a movie with her family. She had worked a 12-hour shift that day and was very tired, but felt that this time was important. During the movie, Tommy reminds her that he has a baseball game tomorrow and asks if she'll be there. Stopping to think, she remembers that she is off this weekend and tells Tommy that she wouldn't miss it for the world.

Fast forward to the following morning. Alice lies in bed a 5:30 am. She'd love to sleep in, but years of 7 am shifts have made her pretty much incapable of it. Resigned to the fact that she is not going to get any more sleep she gets up to start the chores she's been putting off all week. As she walks toward the bathroom, her cell phone rings. Looking at the screen she recognizes the number as that of her hospital. She briefly contemplates ignoring it. This is her day off, after all. As she starts to put the phone back down, she thinks to herself, "It might be important." As guilt overtakes her, she answers the phone. Sure enough, it's her manager, Lisa.

"Alice, I'm so glad you answered. We've had multiple call-ins throughout the hospital and we are really short-staffed. You're such a team player, I knew I could count on you to come in." Lisa says.

For a moment Alice says nothing. She doesn't WANT to go in, but she feels guilty. She doesn't want to be viewed as not being a "Good team player." She feels that being a team player is important. After a brief delay, Alice responds, "Oh, Lisa. This is my day off. Isn't there anyone else you can call?"

Lisa replies, "I mean, yeah, I guess I could call some other people. I just really thought I could count on you."

Remembering Tommy's baseball game, Alice starts to do some calculations in her head. "If I went in, I could leave at 7:00 and go straight to the game." Reluctantly, Alice agrees to go into work. Lisa gives her thanks and hangs up.

With a deep sigh, Alice grabs clothes and heads towards the bathroom for a shower. As she does, her husband walks in and asks who she was talking to on the phone. Alice explains that the hospital is really short-staffed and that Lisa had asked her to come in extra today. Tom reminds Alice of Tommy's baseball game. Alice explains that, if she leaves at 7:00, she can come straight to the ballpark and should be able to get there before the game stars.

Let's fast forward again. It's now 8:00, time for Tommy's game to start. Tommy takes the field, looking over the stands for his mother. Not finding her he sighs and hangs his head a bit while trying not to let his disappointment show. Throughout the game he continues to look into the stands, hoping to see his mom sitting there next to his dad, even though he's pretty sure she's not going to be. At the end of the game, Tommy gathers his gear and heads toward the car with his dad and sister. As they near their car, Alice pulls up. Jumping out she reaches to hug Tommy. Tommy pulls away from her and says, "It's too late, Mom, the game is over. He then jumps in Dad's car, without giving Mom the hug she was reaching for.

Later, after the kids are tucked into bed, Tommy refuses to talk to Alice, despite her apologies. He's heard those before. In their bedroom, Tom asks Alice what happened. "It wasn't my fault," she insists. "Jane was my relief. She can never seem to be on time. Honestly, I don't know why they keep her around." "When was the last time you saw Tommy play," Tom asks. Alice starts to answer but then has to stop and think. She tries hard to remember the last game that he attended. In the end, she tearfully looks at Tom and says, "I can't remember."

Was it Alice's fault that she didn't make it to the game? I mean if Jane had just been there on time, it would have been fine, right? I would argue that Alice didn't miss the game because Jane was late. Rather, she missed the game because she didn't have healthy boundaries in her life. I'm certain that if Alice were to work through the exercises you've worked through in this chapter, she would have placed her role as a mother above her role as a nurse. Yet, when it came down to it, she chose nurse over mother. She would likely not think of it that way, but the reality is that she did not HAVE to work that shift, she could have said no. She didn't choose to miss the game, but she did choose to put herself into a situation that made missing the game possible.

EXERCISE 4

Now, let's look at how you can build healthy boundaries in your life.

Take out that ordered list you made. The one where you put all the different pieces of who you are in order of importance. Take some time to consider each of those pieces. You're going to make a list of ways that you can protect those priorities. You do that by answering these two questions:

- What are some things I need to STOP doing, in order to protect the things I've said are most important in my life?

- What are some things I need to START doing, in order to protect the things I've said are most important in my life?

Looking back at Alice's story, I'm certain that she would have put her role as a mother above her role as a nurse. That being the case, to prevent an event like the one we looked at from happening, she may set a boundary such as this, "I don't pick up extra shifts on days that my kids have events." It's an unfortunate reality that being a nurse will often mean missing some events. I would argue that it doesn't have to be that way, but that's a topic for later. While Alice may still miss some games, if she had this boundary in her life, she would not have missed this game and she likely would miss way fewer of these events.

For me, one of my top priorities is my role as a husband. One of the boundaries I've put in my life to protect that is that I never meet alone with a woman. As a pastor, and even as a nurse, I have had many times when fellow nurses or church members would want to meet with me for mentoring or counseling sort of stuff. I enjoy mentoring people and love doing these meetings. Having this boundary doesn't mean that I can't meet with women. I do meet with them, but I do it in a public place, usually a coffee shop. It costs me a couple of cups of coffee, as I always pay for theirs, but it protects the things that are most important to me.

OK, complete this exercise. Once you've written down a list of things you need to start or stop doing to protect the things that are most important to you, you're ready to move on in the book. Try to name at least 2-3 things for each of those top few items on your list. Oh and, this list is a living document. There may be things that you can't think of now. It's okay to come back to the list later and add or remove items to fit your ever-changing life.

The Restored Nurse Companion Workbook, page 38.

I'm a person who...

Earlier I mentioned Dr. John Delony. If you've not, you really should go check out his podcast/YouTube show. Anyway, another thing that he often has people do is declare "I am..." statements. These statements help us to connect with who we are or with the person we are trying to become. As you work through this book, I'm going to encourage you, in each chapter, to make some of these "I am" statements.

When you first start doing this, it can feel wrong. It can even feel fake or as if you are lying. For instance. One of my "I am" statements is this; "I am a person who takes care of his body." At the time of this writing, I'm sitting at over 300 pounds. At 5'10, that's way too heavy. When I proclaim this statement, it feels like a lie. I look at the mirror and can clearly see that I am not a person who takes care of his body. However, what I'm seeing in the mirror is not evidence of who I am. Rather, it is evidence of who I have been. So, I like to say, "Yes, I have been a person who did not take care of my body. But, now, I am a person who takes care of his body."

Even saying this can feel fake, or unfaithful. The reality is that the difference between the person you were yesterday and the person you are tomorrow is the choices you make today. So, yesterday you may have been a person who did not live by any of the "I am" statements that you are going to make while you work through this book. The good news is that you can make a choice today to become that person. You can declare this new "I am" statement and begin to build a life around that. Over time, the evidence of the person you were will fade and the evidence of the person you are and are becoming will shine through.

One final note about your "I am" statements. To be complete, I believe they need to follow this format "I am a person that _____ by doing ____." This format allows you to spell out not only the person you are becoming, but also how that plays out in your life. So, going back to my "I am" statement about taking care of my body, it would become a series our statements such as:

- I am a person who takes care of his body, by taking my medicine daily.

- I am a person who takes care of his body, by getting at least 30 minutes of exercise every day.

- I am a person who takes care of his body, by drinking 80-100oz of water every day.

I think you get the idea. These don't have to be super specific, but the more specific they are, the more clarity they will bring and the easier they will be to put into action. Remember, these statements, just like the other lists you've made, are part of a living document. Your goals may change, requiring new statements. New seasons of life will require new statements. So, come back to this list at least every 3-6 months and make sure it still fits your life.

EXERCISE 5

Take some time and write some "I am" statements. For inspiration, you can look at the list you made in exercise 3. Thinking back to Alice, she set a new boundary to not work extra when her children have events. So, she might create an "I am" statement that says,

"I am a person that prioritizes my relationship with my children by not working extra shifts on days they have events."

The Restored Nurse Companion Workbook, page 40.

Chapter Three

What is Health

"Dear friend, I pray that you may prosper in every way and be in good health physically just as you are spiritually." 3 John 2.

What is health?

This might seem like a simple enough question, but it's not. In the last chapter, we addressed the question of who you are. We found that while we can quickly answer the question, "Who are you?" the answer can be much deeper than we often think. The same is true with how we might define health.

As a nurse, our first inclination might be to define health as simply the absence of disease. But, is that enough? Consider a young person who is morbidly obese. This person may have not yet developed any of the diseases associated with obesity. Would we say that they were healthy, simply because these diseases haven't developed yet? Or maybe a smoker who's only been smoking for a few years. Are they healthy because they don't have symptoms of COPD yet?

These two examples may be pretty obvious. But, what of a person who is extremely fit and physically healthy, but contemplates suicide regularly? Would we consider this person to be healthy? Sure, their physical health is great, but their mental health is clearly suffering. Or maybe a person whose physical and mental health are good, but their relationships are falling apart. Would we consider them to be truly healthy? Would we only decide a marriage is unhealthy when it starts divorce proceedings?

It seems clear to me that health is much more than simply the absence of disease.

Merriam-Webster gives multiple definitions for health. One states that health is, "the condition of being sound in body, mind, and spirit." I like this one because it shows that health is holistic. It's about more than simply the condition of your body. That is certainly a factor, but it is not the only factor. Another definition they give is, "a condition in which someone or something is thriving or doing well." Thriving certainly sounds like more than simply the absence of disease. How many of us have experienced good health in certain areas of our lives, but still didn't feel like we were thriving?

When I think of thriving in my physical fitness, I don't think of myself running a marathon. For some, this may be the measure. For me it's about walking up the bleachers at the high school I announce football for, without feeling like I'm going to die. It's about being able to get on the floor and play with my grandchildren when they come. I also think about being able to perform my daughter's wedding someday. She's 14 at the time I'm writing this, so I have some time before this happens. I want to be there.

How would I define health?

In defining health, I would start by agreeing with the statements above that health is more than simply the absence of disease. I also really like the Merriam-Webster definition that talked about thriving as a factor in health. Lastly, I would say that health has to encompass all six of the pillars of a restored life. So, for the sake of this book, we will define health as:

"Thriving in one's work health, physical health, mental health, spiritual health, relational health, and financial health."

How do we measure health?

How one measures health may vary greatly depending on who we are asking, what training that person has had, their own experiences, etc. While there are some clear measurements for things like physical or mental health, I will leave those measurements to the experts. Instead, for the sake of this book, I want to focus on habits.

Why habits?

To a great extent our lives, as they currently exist, are a result of our habits. Before anyone starts writing emails or social media posts blasting me for this, let me acknowledge that there are events in our lives that can have a major impact. Still, many areas in our lives are the result of the habits that have gotten us to this point.

I'm overweight because I have a habit of eating too much and not exercising. My wife and I ended up with piles of debt because for years we had a habit of using debt for lots of different things. On the positive side, we have been able to pay off large amounts of that debt because we developed new habits that included not using debt and paying off what we had. For another positive, I have a great relationship with my children and wife, because spending time with them is a habit that I've nurtured for decades.

I truly believe that if we focus on the habits that will move us toward the people we want to be, then we can't help but move in that direction.

Input vs outcome

For many of us, when we are working on a new goal, we focus heavily on the outcome. This makes total sense, the outcome is the reason we are doing the work. Even as I type these words, the program I'm using is counting them in a margin to the right side of my laptop screen. It's tracking my progress toward my goal. When someone is working to lose weight, they may tend to focus on the numbers on the scale.

When someone is paying off debt, they may focus on the amount of money they still owe. While this is valuable and even necessary, to a degree, I think that it is much more important to focus on the things we are doing to reach those goals.

Consider the person trying to lose weight. If this person focuses on the scale, without giving a clear focus to what they are eating, then they will get on that scale every week or month and HOPE that they've done the right things to get the results they desire. However, if they focus on what they eat, then they can get on the scale with confidence that they have done what is necessary. You see, the input will affect the outcome, but the outcome doesn't, necessarily, affect the input.

So, as we get into measuring health in each of the 6 Pillars, we will focus more on the input, the habits. In most cases, we won't even address the outcome goals at all. This is partly because of my strong belief that our lives are the result of our habits. It's also due, in part, to the fact that everyone's outcome goals will be different because our situations are all slightly different. The person who needs to lose 150 pounds has a different goal than the person working to lose 15 pounds. The person with $200,000 in debt has a different goal than the person with no debt, who's trying to save for retirement. One person may have a relational goal of saving their failing marriage, while another may have a good marriage and have a goal of making it even better.

Measuring health in the 6 Pillars

So, how do we measure health in each of the 6 Pillars? We are going to look closely at each of the pillars in the upcoming chapters. For now, know that these measurements are addressed in the Restored Life Assessment located in the appendix of this book, or online at restoringnurses.com/assessment.

As a reminder, the 6 Pillars of the restored life are:

- Work Health

- Physical Health

- Mental Health

- Spiritual Health

- Relational Health

- Financial Health

EXERCISE 6

For this exercise I want you to take some time to think about the 6 Pillars. For each of them, you are going to create a definition of what health looks like in your life. This needs to be personal. It has to come from YOU. If you write down textbook definitions then it will not have the power to keep you moving forward. I also don't care what others think health should look like for your life. I want to know what YOU think health looks like for your life. To help, here are some of mine.

Work Health

- To never dread going to work.

- Doing work I love.

- Doing work that impacts the lives of the people I serve.

Physical Health

- To climb the bleachers without feeling like I'm dying.

- To be able to get on the floor and play with the grandchildren that will come someday.

- To be around to perform my daughter's wedding.

Mental Health

- To believe my worth, regardless of what the people around me may say or do.

- To truly love the man in the mirror, no matter what he might look like.

Spiritual Health

- To know that while I'm not perfect, my life regularly reflects the faith I claim.

- To regularly serve others.

- To trust God in all things, leaning on the Holy Spirit, even when I may feel all alone.

Relational Health

- To be a friend to my children as they enter adulthood and a safe place for them while they are children.

- To pursue my wife, even as I did when we were teenagers.

- To have close friends, like the kind who will help you move, or answer your call at 2 am.

Financial Health

- To be outrageously generous without concern for my bills being paid.

- To be able to order what I want at a restaurant, without looking at the price.

- To know that if I died, my family would be taken care of.

So, how will you define health in each of these six pillars? Once you've made your list, I'd love to see them, if you don't mind sharing. Email your list to me at matt@restoringnurses.com

The Restored Nurse Companion Workbook, pages 44-47.

EXERCISE 7

So, you've identified what you want your life to look like, now let's make a plan to get there. This where Actionable Goals come in. Take some time to consider your Desired Outcomes and what habits you could build, over time, that would move you toward those outcomes.

Now go to page 48 in *The Restored Nurse Companion Workbook and complete this exercise.*

Chapter Four

Work Health

"Am I seriously being written up AGAIN?"

I found myself asking this question, as I faced yet another disciplinary action. I think this was the third time in as many months. This is more than I had been written up in 20 years as a nurse. Had I really gotten that bad, or was this personal? I loved the work I was doing, but I didn't like the person that I was becoming as a result of the way I was being treated. I hated the thought of leaving my patients, but I was pretty sure it was time to move on.

Several years have passed since I left that job. I truly loved the work I did. It may be the most fulfilling work I've ever done as a nurse. But, the work environment wasn't healthy for me and, ultimately, meant I had to leave work I loved to do what was best for me.

What is work health?

When we think of health, work may not be the first thing we think about. Sure, some of us may have thoughts about the negative effects our work might be having on our health, but work health is not something we often think about. When we have discussions of self-care, we may think about work, but usually more along the lines of things we are going to do to get away from our work. This may be vacations, hobbies, nights out, or a wide variety of other things. While these things can certainly be part of a comprehensive self-care plan, they are not directly related to work health.

Many would agree that work is an unfortunate reality of life. I would go so far as to say that work is a good thing. The Bible talks a lot about work. In Exodus, God told the people of Israel that they were to work six days and rest on the seventh. Work was so important that God gave them some specific instructions related to it. Whether you think that work is a good thing or a necessary annoyance, it's important that we strive to have work health.

So, what is work health? Well, to put it simply, it's work that works for you, work that is not harming the other aspects of your health. I've seen way too many nurses stay in an unhealthy work situation much longer than they should have. This happens for a wide variety of reasons. Regardless, work health is attainable, but it may mean making some uncomfortable choices.

Work that is balanced

Work-life balance is a popular buzzword. I can't say it's always been that way, but it certainly has for as long as I can remember. It makes sense. We all have to work, who wouldn't want work that balances with the life you want to live? The problem is that most of us have been looking at work-life balance wrong. Most of us look at work-life balance as a time thing. I think it's something different.

On average nurses in America work 36-48 hours per week. Remember, this is an average, so it includes some working much more than that, and some working less. With 168 hours available every week, that leaves 120-132 hours per week when you are not at work. If we then assume 8 hours of sleep per night, we are left with 64-76 hours per week for our "life". If work-life balance were just a simple math problem, then we should be able to work our three to four 12-hour shifts, get a good night's sleep each night, and still have time for a full life. The problem is that this math equation doesn't take into account the energy that work requires.

The key to work-life balance isn't simply working less or planning better. It's much more complicated than that. To see how you are currently doing in this department, take time to complete the Restored Life Assessment in the appendix of this book, or at restoringnurses. com/assessment.

Consider this question: On average, how many weeks per month do you work over 40 hours?

Work that fits your life

I remember when I was in nursing school. I was in my early 20s, married, with no children. I was determined that my work would never dominate my life. Somewhere along the line, I drifted into a place where my life became more about the work I was doing and less about the life I wanted to live. Sure, the work we do is important, but so is your life outside of work.

I've seen a tendency in nurses to build lives that fit their careers, rather than the other way around. This is probably common in many if not most other fields. I speak of nursing simply because it's the only career I've ever had. If asked, we would say that there are things in our lives more important than nursing, but when we get down to it, our choices might say something different.

Now, you might be reading this and thinking, "No way, Matt, I never do this." Let me ask you a question. How often do you miss family events because of work? How many of your child's performances, games, recitals, etc have you had to miss because you were at work? How often have you calculated the time it would take you to get from work to whatever was going on in your kid's life? What if your relief is late? What if traffic is bad? If you're delayed are you going to miss the show?

The truth is that this is just a reality that nurses have accepted as an inevitable part of being a nurse. What if I told you that I've never missed a performance of either of my kids? What if I told you that, while my son was in the high school band, I was at everything he did? Yep, every concert, every football game, every marching band show, all of it. I don't say this to brag. It's not about me. I say this to say I did it while working full-time as a nurse.

At some point, if you want work health, you are going to have to ask, "Does this job fit my life, or am I trying to make my life fit this job?"

Consider this question: In the past 3 months, how many times have you missed personal/family events because of work?

Work that you love

Listen, I know that nursing is hard. I'm not saying that you should seek out an easy job. Still, let me ask you this, have you ever had work that you loved at a job you hated?

I think back to when I was working at an outpatient cancer center. I truly enjoyed caring for those patients. From educating them about the treatments to helping ease their fears, to even sharing a tear or two with them on the hard days. I truly loved helping these patients get through the difficult moments. I enjoyed laughing with them and watching some of them learn that it was okay to smile and laugh, even amid these dark times.

As much as I love the WORK, there were some factors at the JOB that required me to seek other opportunities. When I talk about work you love, that's what I'm talking about. Work you love CAN be about a great work environment. That certainly helps. However, more than that it is about the work you are doing while you are there. If you don't love the work, then it can be really difficult to attain work health.

Work that fulfills you

Fulfillment is another buzzword that gets tossed around from time to time. A job that is fulfilling, but doesn't feed my family is not a good job. If fulfillment was the only factor in work health, then most of us would likely choose to do something much different than what we are doing. Still, fulfillment does matter.

So, what is fulfillment? Merriam-Webster equates fulfillment with being satisfied. Some might say that work that is fulfilling is work that feeds you. Others may say work that gives you meaning or worth.

Regardless of how you might define it, the question remains, does the work you do fulfill you?

I think it's important that we remember that when I talk about work that fulfills, I'm not talking about your job, but about the work you do while you're there.

Consider these questions: Does my work fulfill me? Does my work give me meaning?

Work that is safe

This one should probably be a no-brainer. Everyone deserves a safe work environment. This is a large part of the reason that unions were formed many years ago in the US. While this should be automatic, it, sadly, isn't. During just shy of 30 years working in healthcare, I have seen a clear decline in the safety of nurses on the job. Acts of violence against nurses, and other healthcare workers have become a regular occurrence. When I was a charge nurse in the ED, I cared deeply about the safety of the people under my charge. This included staff, patients, and even visitors. When it became clear that I no longer had the support of management to do what I needed to do to maintain that safety, I knew it was time for me to move on.

Way too many nurses just accept that violence is "part of the job." It doesn't help that a growing portion of the general population believes this. When an attack against a nurse hits the news or social media, there will inevitably be comments from people outside of healthcare stating "This is what you signed up for." There are absolutely jobs where violence is inevitable. Law enforcement, corrections, military, just to name a few. While we, as nurses, should understand that violence is likely to happen to us, we CANNOT accept it as a normal part of the job. We do not have to work for companies that don't ignore their responsibility to keep us safe. Are you in a place like that? If so, you need to move on. There are plenty of other jobs.

Work that is safe is not just about physical safety. Physical violence most often comes from patients or visitors. While our mental or emotional safety can be threatened by these same people, it quite often comes from providers, managers, administrators, and even the very organizations that we work for. Few of us would openly ignore or allow physical violence, but we accept mental or emotional abuse from these sources regularly without even thinking about it. The truth is that this mental and emotional abuse sometimes has longer-lasting effects than the physical violence we endure as nurses. Most physical attacks on nurses are a single incident from a single attacker. By contrast, emotional or mental abuse may go on for months or even years. You deserve better than that. If you are in a facility that is abusive to you, then I want you to put this book down right now and start looking for another job. Once you've applied for a couple of positions, come back and pick up where you left off, but you will struggle with every concept in this book if you continue in a workplace that is constantly beating you down.

Hear me when I say this. You deserve to be safe, physically, mentally, and emotionally.

Consider this question: Do you feel safe at your job, emotionally, mentally, and/or physically?

Go back to page 45 in *The Restored Nurse Companion Workbook* and review the Desired Outcomes you wrote for Work Health. Ok, now go to page 48 for a refresher on Actionable Goals. Finally, go to page 49 and write some Actionable Goals that will move you toward those Desired Outcomes you wrote down.

Chapter Five

Physical Health

"Have you seen Matt lately? I swear he gets bigger every time I see him."

Chances are that the above conversation has only ever happened in my head. Still, it doesn't change the fact that it's true. Over the years of my nursing career, I have worked hard to take care of everyone else, while mostly ignoring my own physical health. I've gone from being "the big guy" to being morbidly obese on meds for my blood pressure, with a real concern for the state of my blood sugar. All the while, telling patients they needed to make better food choices, exercise more, or lose a little weight.

My story is far from unique. Nurses know what it takes to be physically healthy. Heck, that is literally what we went to school for. Still, so many of us struggle with it. Shift work, stress, and the physical and emotional demands of the job truly make physical health complicated for nurses. Still, it's not impossible.

What is Physical Health?

There exist a number of concrete measures for physical health. While some, such as BMI, may be contested, they are still out there. Even beyond simply measuring weight or body fat, there are things such as blood pressure, and a wide variety of blood tests that can tell us much about our physical health. As mentioned in a previous chapter, it is not my desire to address those measures in this book. There are people way more knowledgeable about such things than me. I will leave those measures to them. Rather, my goal in this chapter is to focus on the habits that will lead us to improved physical health.

So, what is physical health? Well, exactly how a given person defines that may vary from one person to another. For me, as I started a physical health journey, my goal had a few layers:

- No longer need blood pressure medicine.

- Be able to climb the bleachers to get to the pressbox at the high school without feeling like I was going to die.

- Be able to get on the floor and play with my grandchildren, when they come.

- Be around to perform my daughter's wedding.

For you, physical health may mean something different. So, for the sake of this book, we are going to focus on the habits that will help us move towards whatever your measure of physical health is.

Movement

There is a common mistake that many of us make when we decide it's time to take our physical health more seriously. I've seen others make it, and I've made it myself on several occasions. Cognitively we know that we are not going to go from couch potato to marathon runner, or strength competitor. Yet, we often run out, get a gym membership, and start going five days a week. Or, maybe we fancy ourselves a runner. We buy some new running shoes and start hitting the pavement. Whatever our mistake of choice, many of us jump into too great an activity too quickly. I will caveat this by saying that this works for some people. However, for the vast majority of us, this is not going to work.

Not only will this approach likely not work, it often brings more problems than it fixes. This sort of approach puts us at much greater risk for injury. That injury could put us even further back than when we started. It can also lead to discouragement as we attempt things that are too far beyond our capacity. I'm not saying that we shouldn't try hard things. When it comes to physical activity, we absolutely should push ourselves. At the same time, we need to know our limits and understand that pushing too far beyond our current limits can be bad for us.

So, what should we be doing? Well, the goal of this point is simply to move more than we have been. If you're just starting this may be as simple as a 30-minute walk 4-5 times a week. If that's too much, make it 15 minutes and work your way up from there. The point is simply to move more this week than you are used to. Then, next week, move a little more.

Consider this question: How much activity (exercise) do you get per week?

Water

Okay, this is another area where I am not going to tell you exactly how much water you should be drinking. There are as many different opinions on this are there are on just about all the other nutrition, exercise, or personal fitness topics. What I can say with some confidence is that you are probably not drinking enough water right now.

I'm not going to spend a lot of space on this topic, but I want to ask you this: How much water do you drink per day?

Again, the amount you should be drinking depends on who you are talking to. I've heard anywhere from 80-100 ounces, to a gallon, to half your body weight in ounces of water per day. On a side note, I tried that last one once. At the time I was a little over 300 pounds. That means drinking 150 ounces of water per day. I began to rethink this one as I was stuck in traffic on the interstate and nearly wet my pants. If you're able to take in that much and it works for you, great. For me, this was too much. The one thing I will say is to look at the color of your urine. If it is dark, drink more water. The goal isn't necessarily to get it completely clear. Shoot for a pale yellow color.

One more thing I will add regarding water. Consider your activity today, and your plans for tomorrow. Have you been sweating more today than normal? Drink more water. Do you have activities tomorrow that will cause you to sweat more? Then drink more water today. Hydration for tomorrow happens today. By the time you get thirsty tomorrow, you are already behind.

Consider this question: How much water do you drink per day?

Nutrition

This one is even more hotly contended than the water question. There is no shortage of "experts" online willing to tell you all about the things you should or shouldn't eat. In many cases, those so-called "experts" have little to no actual training or education in nutrition. Most of them are trying to sell you something.

Still, other folks on social media have strong opinions about their preferred plan because it worked for them. That's awesome. I'm so glad that the plan worked for them. However, just because it worked for that individual does not mean that it is the perfect plan for everyone. The truth is there is no such thing as a "perfect diet." We all have different needs, not just nutritionally, but in regards to taste, schedule, medical status, and many other factors. I've often heard it said that the best diet plan for you is the one that you will do, and I agree with this... mostly.

There are a few constants that are true, regardless of the diet plan:

- Consuming more calories than you burn will lead to weight gain.

- Most of us don't eat nearly enough vegetables.

- Planning your food will help you reach nutritional goals.

- Sugary drinks taste good, but provide almost no nutritional value while adding a bunch of calories.

So, let me ask you this. How intentional are you about what you eat, and how much you eat?

Sleep

There is a bit of a joke in nursing that says that caffeine should be considered a food group. I've seen memes that state if you are operating on rage, an Oreo cookie, and enough caffeine to kill a horse, then you might be a nurse. Nurses consume a LOT of caffeine. I, personally, love coffee. The reality is that caffeine can't replace a good night's sleep, something most of us don't get enough of.

While the exact recommendations may vary, most agree that an active adult needs between seven and nine hours of sleep per night. How often do you get at least seven hours of sleep? If you're like most of us, it's probably not very often.

It's crazy, there have been so many "gurus" saying that you can operate on less sleep than that. Yes, you can, but for how long? You may be getting less sleep than this and thinking that it is not affecting you. Trust me, it is. It will catch up with you at some point.

Consider this question: On average, how many nights per week do you get 7 or more hours of sleep?

Screen Time

Ooh, I'm gonna hurt some feelings with this one. That's not my intention. But, let me ask you, how much time do you spend in front of a screen? How much time are you in front of a screen at work? How much TV do you watch at home? How much time do you spend scrolling social media on a tablet or phone? If you're like most modern people, you spend a LOT of time in front of a screen.

Just like most of the other things in this chapter, I'm not going to tell you exactly how much screen time is healthy. There are many studies out there with a wide variety of recommendations. What I will say is this, however much screen time you are getting each day, it should probably be less.

Consider this question: How much screen time do you get per day?

Where does physical fitness fit in the Christian life?

Like so many things in life, physical health can become an idol, something we worship. As a Christian, this is something that has to be avoided. So, what does that mean for Christians?

One thing that is clear throughout the Bible is that gluttony is bad. Gluttony can be used to describe an over-indulgence in food or lots of over things. Many verses negatively speak of gluttony. For most of us, obesity is an obvious sign of gluttony. I don't say this to bring guilt. As I write this I'm well into the obese category. Rather, I share this to bring awareness. I'm painfully aware of this sin in my life and it is something I'm working on. If you're in this boat with me, remember God's promises, in Romans 8:1 that, "there is now no condemnation for those in Christ Jesus." God does not condemn us and we have to stop condemning ourselves. At the same time, grace does not mean we can continue to ignore and live in our sin.

On the other side of this, physical health is celebrated throughout the Bible. In 3 John 2, John writes, "Dear friend, I pray that you may prosper in every way and be in good health physically just as you are spiritually."

So, as Christians, we have to take care that physical health or fitness does not become an idol, but it is important to pursue it and even okay to celebrate others as they work to improve it.

Like in the last chapter, go to page 45 in *The Restored Nurse Companion Workbook*, to review the your Desired Outcomes for Physical Health. Then go to page to write some Actionable Goals to get you there.

Chapter Six

Mental Health

"**S**o this is what that feels like."

You may recognize this line from the movie *Sweet Home Alabama*. In this scene, the handsome groom gets left at the altar, just moments before getting married. There's a moment of self-reflection and he says the above quote. For me, this thought came as I was convinced that I was having a nervous breakdown. I had never really experienced anxiety before and, in a single moment, I became afraid of everything. I had always been very confident, but as I woke the next morning, I was suddenly afraid of nearly everything. I couldn't get in elevators, I was afraid to start IVs, even though I had started thousands.

As I prepared for bed, I could feel the now familiar pressure building in my chest. The anxiety was coming. Bedtime became something I dreaded because it was where it all started and every night was a reminder. I would lie in bed and pray myself to sleep, "Lord, give me peace, give me strength." For months I would repeat this prayer, till I fell asleep.

As I write this I realize that I am very close to a decade since that night. In that time, I have learned so much about myself. I have learned what triggers me and, more importantly, I've learned how to avoid my triggers and how to deal with the anxiety when it does come. Many of the things that scared me that next morning no longer scare me. I still experience some anxiety but it is much more rare and, when it does come, I'm better equipped to address it.

My experience that night and in the subsequent days was a catalyst for me to better understand and care for my mental health. While many nurses recognize their need for physical health, many treat their mental health as if it's not a factor. Somehow, in an industry known for caring for others, a stigma has developed in nursing when it comes to mental health. We've got to do better.

One more thought on mental health before we jump into the specifics. PTSD is something we expect from war veterans. However, I once read a study that stated that nurses deal with levels of PTSD similar to those among war veterans. What's worse, this study was done in 2019, before COVID.

Sleep

Ok, I know we already talked about this one in the last chapter. For this reason, I'm not going to spend a lot of time talking about it. I will, however, say that just like sleep affects your physical health, it also affects your mental health. If you are not getting seven to nine hours of sleep per night, on a regular basis, then your mental health is suffering from it.

I'll ask the same question I asked in the last chapter: How many nights per week do you get 7 or more hours of sleep?

Social Media

I think back to when I was a kid. At that time in history, if we wanted to learn about what was going on in the world, we had to wait for the 6:00 news or grab a newspaper the following morning. Moving into my adolescence came cable TV. With this came the ability to get news around the clock. In fact, when something bad happened it was not unusual for news coverage to be all day long. I remember in 1992 when Hurricane Andrew hit south Florida, just a couple hours drive from where I live. We were able to watch news reports of it pretty much whenever we wanted to. Still, it did require that we be near a television. Fast forward a bit more and we get the advent of smartphones and social media. Now we can get near-instant access to news wherever we are and whenever we want it, sometimes even when we don't want it.

This constant dosing of "news" can't possibly be good for us. Especially considering that the only things the mainstream media ever talks about are things aimed at either scaring us, making us angry, or building dissension among the people.

With social media also came the ability for people to say the most horrendous things to others without any repercussions. People could suddenly say things on the internet that they would never say face to face. This has proved to be a contributing factor to increases in anxiety, depression, and even suicide.

All this being said, I'm not saying that social media is a bad thing. However, like screen time, there is a point at which it can become a negative. I'm not going to try to tell you how much you should or shouldn't consume social media. Rather, I'm just going to advise you to be mindful of how much you consume and, if you are like most of us, you should probably cut back a little. This is especially true if you are struggling with any degree of mental health concerns.

Downtime/Rest

Maybe you're reading this one and thinking, "Matt, you already talked about sleep." Yes, I did talk about sleep and this is something different. Sleep can certainly be restful, but that should not be the only time that you rest. Let me ask you this, when was the last time you did nothing? I mean intentionally avoiding any activity.

My wife and I look at vacation very differently. Wherever we go, she is looking for things to do, I want to don't. I know that's a funny way to put it, but I tend to stay so busy DOING that when I go on vacation I want to DON'T for a while. This is not to say that I don't enjoy a game of mini-golf with the fam or some time in the pool or tossing a ball on the beach. I just mean that I want to spend a fair portion of my vacation sitting around with something cold to drink, reading a book.

Consider this question, How many times per month do you take intentional time to rest?

Time outside

This one may seem like a strange one for some folks. Many studies have been done that showed the positive mental health effects of simply being outside. This is one of the factors that contribute to seasonal affective disorder. In locations where the temperature drops significantly in the winter, people tend to spend less time outside and it can lead to negative mental health effects.

So, what do we mean by "time outside"? Well, this can be just about anything. This can be as simple as watching the sun come up from your porch while drinking your morning coffee. This is one of my favorites. It can be going for a walk in the neighborhood or a nearby park. This one is a two-for-one, as it gets you moving as discussed in the previous chapter, as well as getting you outside. Take that walk with friends or family and now it's a three-for-one, as it benefits your relational health as well. More on that later.

Consider this question; How many times per week do you spend time outside?

Personal connections

We were made for connection. In the book of Genesis, we read that God looked at Adam and said that it wasn't good for him to be alone. Adam was surrounded by all the animals that God created and still, God considered Adam to be alone. In response to the loneliness of Adam, God created Eve. Throughout the Bible, we can see the importance of connections with other humans. I love my dog. I take great comfort in her presence, but she is not a person.

The importance of human connection is not limited to the Bible. Throughout our history, we can see it. I think of the movie Castaway. While fiction, it does show the effects of long-term isolation from other people. We live in an interesting time. We are more connected than at any point in history and, at the same time, we are lonelier than ever.

As I write this, I think back to my time working in the ER. I've often wondered how I managed to make it just shy of 20 years in the ER when the average for most people is closer to five years. As I think about it, I realize that a major part of my longevity was due to personal connections. I worked with some great people. But, the connection was more than just a matter of working with good people. I remember something we did regularly. We had a habit of meeting together, outside of work. Every other Friday, we would get off shift,

I was working nights at the time, and meet at a local coffee shop. We would spend hours there hanging out, debriefing from work stuff, or just chatting about our families and our lives.

I'm also reminded of Kathy. Kathy was one of the night shift charge nurses when I first started working at the hospital as a phlebotomist in 1996. She was friendly and helpful. After a year in the lab, I transferred to the ED and Kathy became my charge nurse. Over time she also became my friend and mentor. I remember many shifts, hanging out in the parking lot after work. I would talk, vent really, and she would listen. When necessary, she would provide wise advice.

I tell these stories because they point to the importance of personal connections with others. We must make a regular habit of connecting with other people. I have some incredible friends. Unfortunately, my closest friends live hundreds of miles away. I'm thankful for the technology that allows me to connect with them regularly. They have helped me through some difficult times. Still, these online connections can not take the place of being in person with someone. Even with these close friends, there is something special about the time that we get to spend together in person.

Consider this question: How often do you connect with people outside of work?

Journaling

I remember a pastor I served under once telling me, "Our thoughts untangle when they go from our minds to our fingertips." He was talking about the importance of writing our thoughts down. This quote was not his. It came from a man named Dawson Trotman. His exact quote was, "Thoughts disentangle themselves when they pass through lips and fingertips." What he's telling us is that when we talk about our thoughts and feelings or write them down, they become disentangled and easier for us to understand and manage.

I'd love to tell you that journaling is something I do regularly and how it has affected my life. Well, that wouldn't be entirely true. While it's not something I do regularly, it is something that I have done off and on since I was in high school, over 30 years ago. During difficult times in my life, journaling has been a way to clear my mind, to get thoughts that were bouncing around in my head under control or out completely. It gave me a way to process what was happening in my life.

I still have journals that I wrote decades ago. In recent years I have dug up those old journals and started transcribing them into an electronic form. I've done this so that I can have these thoughts and feelings for years after the paper they are written on or the ink they are written with may have deteriorated. It's been so interesting to read through these old journals as I type them into my computer. It's fascinating to see the issues that I have faced in the past, and how I've overcome them and grown through them.

Consider this question: How often, on average, do you do journaling of any sort? (gratitude, prayer, or regular journaling of events and feelings)

I think you know what to do now. Go to page 46 in *The Restored Nurse Companion Workbook* and review your Desired Outcomes, then go to page 50 and write some Actionable Goals.

Chapter Seven

Spiritual Health

I remember when I first felt called to become a pastor. I didn't know what God might have planned and I didn't know what this call would mean for my future. One thing I did know was that I was not where I needed to be spiritually. I had grown up in the church, in the churches my father pastored. Sadly, like so many people who have been in church for years, I had more knowledge than I had true spiritual maturity. I set out on a journey to turn the faith that I had inherited from my parents into my own faith. I have worked since then to grow stronger in that faith

This story reflects my spiritual journey as a Christian. At the same time, I think it reflects the spiritual journey of people from a wide variety of faith traditions and even those that call no faith tradition their own. A great many people do claim a given faith tradition. However, many claim none and would consider themselves non-religious. At the same time, many of these people would consider themselves to be spiritual. I truly believe that we are all spiritual creatures, regardless of our religious beliefs or affiliations. As such, spiritual health is an important part of taking better care of ourselves.

Faith Community

As mentioned in the last chapter, time with people is important to our mental health. It's also important to our spiritual health. I'm not well versed in other faith traditions, but the Bible has many references to the importance of gathering together with our faith community. For me, as a Christian, this means regular attendance at a Sunday worship service. For other Christians, it may mean gathering at different times and in different places. Regardless of what that gathering looks like, it's important for our spiritual health that it happens.

However, spiritual health and gatherings with our faith community are not limited to those corporate gatherings that we are familiar with. These gatherings are important, but for strong spiritual health, you need to be with people who share your spiritual beliefs more than just once a week. The good news is that spending time with these people can also serve the mental health needs we discussed in that chapter, as well as the relational health needs we will talk about in the next chapter.

Consider this question: How often do you spend time with your faith community or people with similar beliefs and values?

Service to Others

There is something powerful about setting your own needs aside to serve others. As I look back on my own life I realize that I have served others since as early as my teenage years. For me, like many other nurses, this is something that comes naturally. Heck, for many of us, this is the very thing that led us to become nurses, even if we didn't know it at the time.

Many studies have shown the positive effects of serving others. I'm not going to take the time to reference those specific studies here, as that's not the point of this book. Maybe my next book will be a bit more scientific. Regardless, the benefits of serving others are very real. In Christianity, as well as many other faith traditions, service is an important part of living out our faith. I would argue that it is also an important part of our spiritual health, regardless of how you might label your spirituality.

As nurses, we serve each other and our patients every day. While this is hugely beneficial for our spiritual health, it may not be enough. You see the unfortunate reality is that the stresses we experience as a nurse may negate some of the benefits of serving others through our work. For this reason, we need to seek out opportunities to serve others outside of our work. This can be a wide variety of things. Just look around your city, neighborhood, or within your faith community and see what opportunities exist. Then get involved.

Is service demeaning?

I once asked the question on TikTok, "Is nursing a calling?" In this video, I shared my belief that nursing is not a calling, but that service to others is. Some folks disagreed and said that for them nursing was a calling. I am certainly not arguing that it can't be a call for some. That's a discussion for another day. One person, however, replied and said that service to others was demeaning. This I don't agree with. The idea of us being servants can certainly be used to demean us. I would most definitely agree that many C-Suite executives, physicians, and others look at us as less than themselves. I can see where these people look at us as "servants" could be demeaning. However, I would argue that the misuse of this term and action does not make the very act of service a negative.

To anyone who might think that service to others is demeaning, let me ask you this. Do you ever eat at restaurants? You know, the kind that have "servers". Do you consider yourself better than the man or woman that is serving you? If you do, then you're wrong... and you're a jerk. Most of us would never consider the person serving us to be less than us, simply because they are serving us. Why then would someone consider themselves to be less when they are the one serving others?

The truth is that we all serve people every day. When my wife cooks me breakfast or packs my lunch, she is serving me. When I take out the trash, mow the grass, fix a wide variety of things around the house, or wash her truck, I am serving my wife. When my wife and I volunteer with our children's high school marching band, we are serving our children and the many others in that organization.

No, service is not demeaning.

Consider this question: How often do you take part in some sort of service to others (outside of work)?

Generosity

This one might ruffle some feathers. When we feel like we don't have enough money for ourselves, it can be hard to think of giving part of what we've got to others. However, just like with service to others, there are real benefits to generosity. As a Christian, I give 10% of my income to the local church. Now, before you go there, I understand that opinions on how much we are "supposed" to give vary greatly. For me and my family, 10% is what we have felt led to do, so it is what we do.

While I think it's important to give to a local faith community that you are an active part of, generosity doesn't have to come in that form. I remember a pastor I worked with, the same one I mentioned earlier when I talked about journaling. He once gave a message on generosity. He said that, as he had been preparing the message, studying and praying over it. He felt led to add a new generosity habit. He put an envelope in the glove box of each of his cars. In this envelope, he always kept $10 - $20 in various bills. He did this so that when he saw someone at a red light asking for money, or in another situation if he felt led to give, he was ready. Whatever form your generosity comes in, seek out opportunities to be generous to others.

Consider this question: How often do you donate money to your church or other charitable organization?

Bible reading and study

Few would argue that exercise is an important part of our physical health. When we set out on a physical health journey, this is often one of the first things we think about. However, when it comes to spiritual health, we will often ignore the importance of reading and studying our Bible. For Christians, the Bible is the source of everything we believe. For many other faith traditions, there is some sacred text. It is crucial to our spiritual health that we spend time in our sacred texts, whatever they may be.

Consider this question: How often do you read/study your Bible?

Gratitude

Gratitude is kinda the unsung hero of spiritual health. The truth is it has great benefits to mental health as well. So, what is gratitude? How do we intentionally practice gratitude?

Let's start with what gratitude is. For the sake of this book, we're going to look at two ways that gratitude manifests. It can be expressed as being grateful for others. As a nurse, I believe it's so important that we are intentional about showing gratitude for the people we work with. This can be other nurses, CNAs/tech, housekeeping, nutritional services, anyone. This not only helps with our working relationships with our colleagues but also helps us to think beyond ourselves, which is one of the benefits of gratitude.

Gratitude can also be manifested in being thankful for the things you have. I'm thankful for my wife and my kids. I'm thankful for some close friends, both the local ones and the ones hundreds of miles away. I'm thankful for a faith community that gives me a place to worship, grow, and serve others. I'm even thankful for the job I have. Not only because it helps me provide for my family, but it also provides an opportunity to do something I love doing and to grow as a nurse and person.

So, how do we practice gratitude? Well, as mentioned above, it can be as simple as saying, "Thank you," to the people around us. This is a great place to start. However, it doesn't have to and shouldn't end there. Gratitude journaling is a great habit that can benefit your spiritual health and can help your mental health as well. This can be as simple as taking time, each day, to write 3-5 things you are grateful for. If you'd like, you can expand it from there to include writing why you are thankful for these things.

Consider this question: How often do you intentionally practice gratitude?

Prayer

As a Christian, prayer is a normal part of daily life. At least it SHOULD be. As mentioned before, this is not a practice unique to Christianity. Many faith traditions include an aspect of prayer. Even those who deny religious affiliation, but aspire to grow spiritually, can often find prayer to be of value.

Sadly, for many Christians, prayer is something we neglect till we face difficulties. Certainly, prayer is powerful in those times, but it is also great when things are going well.

Imagine for a moment being married and only speaking to your spouse when things are bad. This doesn't sound like much of a relationship to me. Or, how about a close friend that you only called when your life was falling apart? In either case, this would not be much of a relationship. Our relationship with God is much like this. If we only talk to God when things are bad, then what sort of relationship do we truly have with Him?

Here's the good news about prayer. We often think of prayer as requiring a certain posture or place. We picture prayer as happening with our eyes closed, kneeling, and heads bowed. While prayer can certainly look like this, it can also look like driving down the road, eyes open, talking with God.

Consider this question: How often do you pray?

> Review your Desired Outcomes on page 46 of *The Restored Nurse Companion Workbook*, then write Actionable Goals on page 50 for Spiritual Health.

Chapter Eight

Relational Health

My Son's afraid of me!

This was my thought as I looked into the eyes of my son. Once again I had cut into him, yelling about something that none of us can even remember. As my beloved son looked up at me, I may as well have been a wild bear rearing up to attack. I had not laid hands on anyone in my family, but I could see that the emotional damage was just as harmful... maybe worse. I can still see the look of fear on his face. Worse than seeing that fear was realizing that I was the object of his fear.

When I was angry, they got scared and I was angry all the time!

Something had to change

Not only was I angry all the time, but my family was suffering as a result of it. This realization had me seeking help. This help came in the form of a counselor. Yes, I know this sounds more like a mental health story than one about relational health, but stay with me.

When I first started meeting with my counselor I knew nothing except that I was angry, like all the time. I also knew that I had to do something about it, but I had no idea how to do that or what might have been the cause. Through working with my counselor, I discovered a link between the current time in my life and my childhood. You see, my parents were not very present in the things that I did. Whether it was baseball or band when I got a little older. I was never really very good at baseball, but I still wanted them there. Band, however, was a completely different story. Not only was I good at it, it was my life in high school. It remained an important part of my life into college and even still today.

I can still see, in my mind, the site of the stands at the football field. I can see myself scanning those stands, hoping to see my parents, not believing they'd be there, but hoping. I have a similar memory of the high school auditorium as the marching band turned into a concert and jazz band. Again, I'm looking at the faces in the crowd only to find they are not there. This was certainly not always the case, but more times than not.

It was from these experiences that my anger came.

Now, hear me when I say that I love my parents. They did so many things well but in this one thing, they missed the mark. I'm not angry with them and I'm grateful to have them as parents.

Family Meals

I love the show Duck Dynasty. It's been off-air for several years now, but it's still a great show. Hmm, It might be time to binge it again. Anyway, if you don't know Duck Dynasty, it follows the Robertsons a group of duck-hunting, God-loving, self-proclaimed rednecks. In each episode, we see the Robertson family along with others connected with them as they live their lives. Each episode ends with the family around the dinner table enjoying time together.

My wife enjoys Duck Dynasty, but not as much as I do. However, we both love the show Blue Bloods. It tells of the fictional lives of a family of New York City Police officers. During almost every episode, the family will gather for Sunday dinner. They take that time to kinda debrief from their week, talk about what's going on in their lives or just enjoy being in the presence of people they love and who love them.

As we watched episode after episode of this show, we were inspired to push for a similar tradition in our own home. Our son was getting ready to graduate from high school and we knew that before we knew it, he would be moving out. We had always been pretty good about eating meals around the table during the week. We worked to make regular Sunday dinners a thing for our family. As I write this, our son is married and he and his wife come over pretty much every weekend for a meal, to play games, or just to hang out.

Consider this question: How often do you share a meal as a family, around a table?

Spouse/Partner

Life is busy. This becomes especially true once you have kids. Early in their life, they require so much care. I mean they literally can't feed themselves, dress themselves, or anything. As they grow, they become more independent, but they also become busy. We trade changing diapers for driving them to dance or soccer practice. Somewhere between dirty diapers and soccer balls, we may wake up and realize that we don't know the person that we have chosen to spend the rest of our lives with, our spouse.

For some, it is when our kids are grown and no longer in the home that we make the realization that we don't know each other. Worse, in some cases, we are not even sure if we still like this person. Sure, we love them, but we are not sure if we like them anymore.

Whether you have young children, your children are grown, or you don't have any children at all, you must be intentional about spending time with your spouse/partner. This doesn't mean simply sitting near one another while the TV plays and you each scroll through social media on your phones.

So, what does count? Well, it can be a regular date night. This doesn't have to be something super expensive. It can be a trip to your favorite restaurant or a simple trip to McDonalds. Not that McDonalds is as cheap as it once was. Spending time with your spouse can be as simple as a walk in your neighborhood, or a nearby park. It can be sitting on the porch for morning coffee, or an evening drink. The point isn't so much the specific activity. Rather, it's about spending time together.

Consider this question: How many times, per month, do you intentionally set aside time to spend with your spouse/partner?

Your Children

If you have children, spending time with them is at least as important as spending time with your spouse. The big difference is that we have limited time to be with our children. In what seems like a blink of an eye, our children are grown, moved out, and building their own lives. Most parents want to be part of that new life that their children are building but fail to realize that the life you want with your adult children starts when they are still truly children.

For me, this means that I am at pretty much everything that my kids do. Every recital, every marching band performance, every concert. Our son was in the high school band and our daughter is now. Since our son was a sophomore, 7 years ago, the band's trailer has been behind my truck for pretty much every trip it took. I don't say this to brag and I'm certainly not saying that you have to do this. However, it is important that you are at these things as frequently as you can.

Your children will not remember the expensive gifts you bought them, or the fancy car you drove. What they will remember is the times that you were at their games, recitals, concerts, etc, or the fact that you weren't.

In my house, another thing that we do to stay connected is play games. During our family dinners, we play games. Every other Saturday I play Dungeons and Dragons with my son, daughter, daughter-in-law, and whoever else wants to join us. Yes, I'm a nerd. Heck, we enjoy playing games so much that we have a TV hanging in our dining room for keeping score or adding visuals to our DND sessions. These activities may or may not be your style. That's ok. This is what works for my family. The point is that you do things to spend time with your children.

One final note on this. Just like you need to find time to be alone with your spouse, you need to make it a point to be with your kids. Like with your wife, this can be expensive, low-cost, or even completely free. There is a common belief that "quality time" can make up for a lack of quantity. Big events or fancy vacations can never take the place of simply being with them. Quantity is much better than "quality". When our son was in high school, I drove him to school every day. We were only a couple miles from the school, so the drive was just a few minutes long. Still, we had some of the best discussions during the short drives. While the individual drives were short, the fact that we repeated it 5 days a week for a few years made each short drive add to all the previous ones. When our daughter was in elementary school I did the same for her. When she moved on to middle school, I picked her up from school most days. Much like with our son, these short trips to or from school became great times to chat about such a wide variety of things and, more importantly, to grow in our relationship. It wasn't until sometime after I no longer needed things for our kids that I learned how much they both appreciated and enjoyed the time we spent together on these short drives.

As I mentioned earlier, our son is married and building his own family. This means no more short trips to school. Now, this time together looks different. Now it means meeting at our favorite coffee shop hanging out and chatting. Sometimes we talk about deep life stuff. Other times we'll spend hours talking about Dungeons and Dragons. Yeah, my son is a nerd too. The point is that even as our kids grow up and move out, they still need us, and being intentional about spending time with them still matters.

Consider this question: How many times, per month, do you intentionally set aside time to spend with your child/children?

Time Away

This is another one that might upset some folks, but here goes. As important as it is to spend time WITH our family, it's also important to spend time away from them. Years ago, this was easy. I was working nights in the ED, working three 12-hour shifts. This meant that I had time to spend alone. So, for a few years, I played golf 2-3 times a week with some guys from work. I was never really very good at it, but I had fun hanging out with these guys. If I'm honest, more recently this is something I've not been good at.

Why is this important? Well, part of it is the mental health aspect that we talked about in a previous chapter. It's more than that though. You see, this entire chapter is about relationships. Building them and maintaining them. This matters because it helps you to develop and maintain an identity outside of your role as husband, wife, mother, or father. Those roles are all important parts of who you are, but they are not all of who you are.

So, think of the friends you have locally and look for ways to spend some time with them. If you don't have any friends that you regularly hang out with, reach out to others that you know who could become good friends. Invite one out to coffee or maybe to grab a meal. Your friendships have to start somewhere. You may find that the people you reach out to are as hungry for this sort of time as you are.

Consider this question: How often do you spend time with friends, with or without your spouse/partner?

Communication

One last thing to talk about regarding relational health is communication. All too often we settle for a very basic form of communication when it comes to our friends and families. I understand why this is for many of us. Opening up and being completely honest can be difficult. I have distinct memories of the looks on some people's faces as I opened up and shared honestly about what I was feeling. I don't know if it's because I'm a man. I don't know if it's because I'm big. I don't know if people are uncomfortable seeing a man cry. Or maybe people have just become uncomfortable with hearing ANYBODY share honestly.

While it can be difficult sharing our own thoughts, hearing the true thoughts of those we care about can also be difficult to hear. Our past experiences from childhood, work, or even our past experiences with our spouse or children can color how we receive the words they say to us. As a result, it can color the way we respond, even when we don't intend for it to.

I'm far from an expert on this topic, so I won't say much more about it. I just end this chapter by saying this, work to learn how to communicate well with the people you care about.

> Review Desired Outcomes on page 47 of *The Restored Nurse Companion Workbook.* Then write some Actionable Goals on page 51.

Chapter Nine

Financial Health

$ 200,000 in debt, not even including the house!

That's where I found myself as I was approaching my 45th birthday. I guess you could say I was having a midlife crisis. How could this have happened? As my wife and I looked at this enormous pile of debt, we knew exactly how it had happened. We had owned more cars than the years that we'd been married and we had been married almost 25 years at that point. We had made good money and had spent even more. Thinking that my 50th birthday was quickly coming, I was physically ill at the thought of hitting that mark with this much debt, little savings or retirement, and no plan for changing it.

This must be what it feels like to drown, only instead of water, I was drowning under the weight of money I owed to other people, and didn't have.

I'd love to tell some amazing story of how we squeezed our budget to the bare minimum, how we got extra jobs, how we sold everything except the children and the dogs and paid off all that debt in like two years. That would be a lie. However, in a little over 3 years since then, we have paid off over $100,000 of it and have built habits that are moving us towards paying off the rest and achieving the rest of our financial goals.

Your financial story may not look exactly like ours, but for many nurses, it's a similar story. In this chapter, I'm going to introduce some habits that begin you on a road toward financial health. Much of what I talk about in this chapter I've learned from Dave Ramsey. I highly recommend reading his book *The Total Money Makeover* and checking out the website ramseysolutions.com

Budgeting

I know, for many this is nearly a curse word. Honestly, it was much the same for my wife and me Budgeting kind of feels like dieting. Dieting often means greatly limiting what or how much you eat. Dieting often means a list of things you CAN'T eat. Dieting is also often something that we think we should do, but don't want to.

Budgeting can have that same feel. It can feel like some outside force telling you what you can and cannot do with the money YOU earned. My wife and I felt like this. However, what we found was that proper budgeting was quite the opposite. We found that budgeting gave us permission to spend. For the first time in over 20 years of marriage, we had money in savings for things such as pet care, auto maintenance, medical, kid's activities, and more. In the past, those things had always ended up being a "surprise" financial burden. Now, there was money sitting in a separate account ready for when this stuff came up.

I'm a giant nerd who loves spreadsheets. So, budgeting for me meant building a big, fancy spreadsheet that we enter our pay and our expenses and it automatically does all the math for us. There are also a bunch of budgeting apps both online and for your phone or tablet. My personal favorite is the Every Dollar app from Ramsey Solutions (no, I'm not in any way getting paid to push their products, I just happen to really like them.) As cool as these things are, you can still just sit down with pen and paper and work it out.

Start with your income. From there right down all your expenses. I'd recommend logging into your bank and looking over all transactions for the past month or two. Look for any regular expenses that are coming out that you might not think about. Now do the math. Be sure to include things like groceries, gas, and any other regular expenses that might not be an actual "bill".

This exercise will let you know where you are starting. From there I would recommend looking to see what items in your current budget you might be able to save money on. This could mean finding ways to lower certain expenses or eliminating them completely. I'll leave those specific decisions up to you, but you do need to give it some thought.

Life Insurance

I know this one is a bit morbid, but here's the deal. We are all going to die. As a nurse, I can almost guarantee that people are depending on your income. What happens to those people if you die? Can they live off what money they might be already making? Do you have enough in savings to support them after you're gone? This is what life insurance is designed to do. No, it's not designed to make your kids, spouse, or partner rich when you die. It's there to make sure that, if you were to die, they would be taken care of.

<u>What kind of insurance do you need</u>? I know that some are going to disagree with this, and that's okay. I believe that what you need is term life insurance. Sure, the insurance salesman is going to try to sell you whole life or some other product that tries to act like both an investment and life insurance. For starters, let your investments be investments and your insurance be insurance. They will both perform much better that way. Term life not only provides you the coverage you need, while you need it, but it is much less expensive than some of the other life insurance products on the market.

<u>How much insurance do you need</u>? This is another one that can vary greatly depending on who you ask. Dave Ramsey recommends 10-12 times your current annual income. Why this amount? Remember that the purpose of this money is to replace your income if you were to die. An amount of 10-12 times your income can be invested in the stock market, experiencing 8-12% growth per year. This would allow your family to replace your income simply on the annual earnings of that investment, without ever having to touch the initial investment amount.

Emergency Fund

If you're like my wife and I for the first part of our marriage, the thought of an emergency fund was laughable. We could barely pay all our bills, much less set aside money for emergencies. Now, however, we take great comfort in that money sitting in a savings account, just in case we need it. Truth is, in the years since we started this, we have only had to use any portion of that money on one or two occasions. As we learned to budget and anticipate upcoming needs, we were able to save up and cash flow almost all of the stuff that came up.

How much should you save for this? Well, this is going to depend on where you are at in your journey. If you, like us, still have debt, then what Dave Ramsey recommends is a $1000 "starter" emergency fund. The truth is that this is NOT enough. I know that, you know that, and so does Dave. For many of us, however, it is far more money than we have ever had in our savings for an extended period. The other truth about this is that most of the unexpected things that come up can truly be covered by this. No, you're not going to completely replace your A/C system for this money, but you can probably get the A/C company to patch it up and keep it running long enough for you to save up enough for the bigger work. This amount is also designed to cause a little bit of anxiety with the hope that it will push you to get your debt paid off.

Once you've got all your debt paid off, except the mortgage, it's time to get a real emergency fund. This fund should be three to six months of your monthly expenses. Notice that I did not say of your monthly pay. This is just your expenses. If you lost your job tomorrow what is the bare minimum it would take to keep your house running for three to six months? This is the amount you want to save up. The idea with this isn't simply that it could replace your income if you lost your job. It could do that, but it should also be enough to replace that A/C system we talked about earlier, get that big car repair, or cover any other unexpected expenses.

Be careful that this fund does not become something other than an emergency fund. This is not a bass boat fund or a new car fund. This is for unexpected expenses only. If you want those other things, save up for them and get them, but don't use this money for that.

Retirement

Depending on your age this is likely something you rarely think about, or something you think about a lot. As I rapidly approach 50 years old, it is something I think about quite a bit. If you're young and don't think you should be thinking about this, I'll simply say this, start thinking about it. I remember reading an article when I was in my 20s that said someone 25 years old could invest as little as $100 per month and retire at 65 with a million dollars. Obviously, the longer you wait, the higher the required investment becomes to reach that same goal. So, if you're young consider giving up a night out, or a few lattes and start investing with that money instead.

How much should you invest? This depends. As I mentioned earlier, the younger you are, the less you have to invest to reach your goals. The amount also depends on your goals. I will likely work in some capacity well beyond the age of 65. I just can't see myself sitting around not working. I mean no disrespect for anyone who does that, but I will likely always be doing work of some sort. This being the case, I might not need quite as much as the person who plans to quit work and spend all their time traveling. There are some great retirement calculators out there. I recommend checking one of them out. My favorite is at, you guessed it, ramseysolutions.com

Congratulations, you've made it to the last of the Actionable Goals. So, go to *The Restored Nurse Companion Workbook*, one more time. Turn to page 47 to review your Desired Outcomes for Financial Health. Then jump to page 51 to write Actionable Goals.

Chapter Ten

Conclusion

Nursing is hard

Y ou don't need me to tell you that nursing is hard. You also don't
need me to tell you that you need to take better care of yourself. We see people on their absolute worst days. We help people get
through some of their most difficult moments, often without anyone
to help us get through ours. We see enough death and pain to drive
most people crazy. If we're honest, it's even driving us a little crazy.

At the same time, nursing is beautiful. We get to share some of
life's most amazing moments with people. There are few things in life
as fulfilling as making a chemotherapy patient smile or, God forbid,
laugh. I'll never forget the day that my chemo patient looked up at me,
smiling, and said, "You make chemo easy." I'll never forget the little girl
who saw me from across the ER lobby and yelled, "That's my nurse!"
Just a couple of days before she was screaming in fear and pain as she
had badly cut her hand. Due to her autism, she struggled to connect
with people and to express how she was feeling in that moment other

than simply screaming. Somehow, she and I DID connect. To her, I was not just A nurse, I was HER nurse.

Yes, nursing is hard but it's also beautiful.

While you don't need me to tell you that nursing is hard, or that you need to take better care of yourself, I think there are some things that I DO need to tell you.

- It is not selfish to take care of yourself.

- It's ok to say no.

- It's better to feel guilty over having said no, than to grow resentful because you said yes.

- You have value.

- You deserve to be cared for.

- You MUST care for yourself, or it will impact how well you can care for everyone else.

These are just a few of the messages I wish I could tell every nurse and convince them of.

No longer forgotten

In Chapter 1 I talked about an old Corvette sitting in a barn, covered with a tarp, plus dust and other things. I think that many nurses feel just like that old Corvette, ignored, forgotten, and broken down. It's true that our employers, our industry, and even many of the people we serve have forgotten about us. Somehow we went from "heroes" during the height of the COVID pandemic to literally being put in jail.

I SEE YOU!

Please hear me when I say that I see you. I see the amazing work you do for patients, many of whom will not only fail to appreciate what you do but will abuse you verbally and often even physically. I see you sitting in the car before work, struggling to get up the motivation to enter the building. I see you crying in the bathroom so that nobody will see you. I see taking a longer route home after another crazy shift because you just aren't ready to be home yet, or don't want to carry the trauma and drama from work home to your family

I SEE YOU!

You deserve this

In the past year or so, I've seen an alarming number of people say that as nurses, you chose the job and, therefore, have chosen the abuse and mistreatment that have become a daily part of the job. That is simply not true. You don't deserve the abuse from patients, visitors, managers, or admins. You don't deserve the working conditions that are neither safe for us nor your patients.

What you do deserve is a life you want to live. You deserve work that is healthy. You deserve a body that is healthy. You deserve mental and emotional health. You deserve spiritual health. You deserve healthy relationships. You deserve health in your finances.

You deserve to be cared for, even if you have to do it yourself.

This is YOUR journey

I live a little bit outside of Orlando. If I were to ask 10 people the best way to get from my house to Daytona Beach, I'd likely get 7 different responses, maybe more. Each of those people giving their opinions would likely be completely convinced that their way was the best. The truth is that each of the potential routes has its advantages and disadvantages. When it comes to your health journey, there are a ton of "experts" willing to tell you their plan and why it is the absolute best plan. They're also usually more than happy to sell you something.

It's important to remember that your health journey is just that, YOUR JOURNEY. This means it may look quite different from other people. It also means that your goals are going to be different, and that's okay.

Progress over perfection

If you're like most people, including me, when you set out on a personal health journey of any sort, you approach it like an excited little boy, on the first day of summer, doing a cannonball into the deep end of the pool. The problem is that sometimes he doesn't know how to swim. And, even if he does, he may not be ready for the deep end. The much wiser approach would be to start at the stairs, in the shallow end, and progress from there.

Just like that child, you run enthusiastically into this new life you're trying to build. I LOVE your enthusiasm, but you might not be ready for the deep end. This is why I recommend an approach much more like walking down the stairs, rather than a cannonball in the deep end. All too often I think we aim for perfection. Then, when we miss the mark, we become frustrated and quit.

Rather than perfection, I encourage you to focus on progress. You see, perfection is a goal we can not reach. However, progress is something we can aim for and reach every day. Think of it like this. If one of your goals is to lose weight and you averaged just one pound per week, at the end of the year you would have lost 52 pounds! Sure, we'd all like to lose it faster than that, but I don't think any of us is going to look back on a 52-pound loss and be upset about it, even if it took longer than we would have liked.

It's about habits

As I said in a previous chapter, I firmly believe that the vast majority of the way our lives currently are is the result of the habits we have lived with up to this point. I am overweight because I have had a long habit of overeating. I'm out of shape because my habits have involved more time on the couch than exercising. I've got debt because my habit used to be to spend more than I made and borrow whatever I could. As you can see, my life is largely a result of the habits I've lived with. Yours is too.

Now, there are certainly circumstances outside of our control that happen, having a profound impact on our lives. Loved ones die. Spouses cheat. Companies close. Pandemics hit the world. These things happen and can have a HUGE impact on our lives. Still, if we are honest with ourselves, most of where we are now is a result of our past habits.

The good news is that habits can have the same effect on your future life that they have had on your past. You see, it was not any single event that made me fat, but rather a long series of habits. In the same way, there's no single event that is going bring me to a healthy weight, but rather a long series of habits that will take me from where I am to where I want to be. Even something like weight loss surgery still requires that we learn new habits. Otherwise, you might very well lose a lot of weight only to find that you gain some, or all of it back.

You CAN do this

If you're anything like me there is a terrible little voice inside your head that is working against you. That voice says the most awful things to me. Mostly it just works to try to convince me that I can't reach the goals I have set for myself. You might be hearing a similar message from your inner voice. Well, it's a lie. You CAN do this.

How do I know? I know because you're a freaking NURSE!! Nursing school is hard. Some studies have shown nursing degrees to be among the most difficult degrees to obtain, and you DID it. That's reason number one that I believe you can do this.

Do you want to know another reason why I believe this? Because I have spent nearly 30 years working with nurses and over 20 years working as one. I have seen nurses do the most amazing things for other people. If you can do it for everyone else, you can do it for yourself.

One last thought

I might be repeating myself with this one, but it's worth saying again and it's the thought I want to leave you with. When I have asked nurses about their biggest barriers to self-care one of the answers that comes up over and over again is guilt. We give so much of ourselves to everyone else, yet feel guilty when we try to give ourselves that same level of care, or even just a portion of it.

You deserve the same care you give to others. The unfortunate reality is that if you don't, at some point, start caring for yourself, it will affect the way you care for everyone else. This includes the people you care about, family and friends, not just your patients. I don't say this to make you feel guilty. Heck, we do this to ourselves well enough.

Rather, I say it in hopes of releasing you from your guilt over taking care of yourself. Rather than being selfish, self-care actually makes you BETTER at caring for others. You see, it benefits you and the people you care for.

Still, let's suppose for a moment that there was no direct connection between you caring for yourself and the care you give everyone else. Even if the only person who benefited from you taking care of yourself was you, YOU STILL DESERVE IT! Now, get out there and do it.

One last thing. If you are anything like me, you need to see some progress to keep from getting discouraged and wanting to quit. Starting on page 53 in *The Restored Nurse Companion Workbook,* you'll find pages for each of the pillars to bring your I Am statements, Desired Outcomes, and Actionable Goals together. Plus, you'll see space for Measures of Success.

Measures of Success are the things that you are going to look at to be able to tell if your Actionable Goals are working. You're going to measure these periodically to see how things are changing.

How often you measure them can vary. For instance, going back to my Desired Outcomes for Physical Health. One of them was to lose 50 pounds. This one I can easily measure daily if I want to. However, I can't go to that football stadium every day and run those stairs. So, that one will have to be measured less often. Or, I might find some other place in the community or even at work where I can measure this. Maybe I climb a flight or two of stairs at work every week or two and see how I feel, or how much my heart rate changes.

> Now, go to the workbook and complete the pages for each of the Pillars. Use this as a starting point to know where you are now as well as a picture of where you are going. I can also serve as a map for the journey between here and there.

Want to work with me?

My passion for helping nurses restore their lives goes well beyond this book or the ones that will follow it in the future.

Speaking: I'd love to speak at your event, or to your nursing group. Learn more at restoringnurses.com/speaking

Coaching: If you're ready to start restoring your life and want a little extra help and encouragement, I'm here for you. Visit restoring nurses.com/coaching to learn more.

Community: The Restoring Nurses Plus Community is a place for nurses who are all journeying towards a restored life. Here you will find community, training, and coaching from me.

Just have questions: I'm here for that too. Feel free to email me anytime at matt@restoringnurses.com.

Chapter Eleven

Appendix A - The Gospel

As I mentioned earlier in this book, I am an ordained pastor. While I never want to try to force my beliefs on anyone, I didn't want to wrap up this book without giving anyone reading this book the opportunity to hear about Jesus' love for them.

If you are not interested, no worries, you can skip this section and move on to Appendix B where you will find the Restored Life Assessment for nurses.

If you're still reading, then I'm going to assume you are interested in hearing about Jesus' love for you.

The Gospel

The message of Jesus' love for us is something Christians call The Gospel. Translated literally, "gospel" means good news. This is because we truly believe that it is good news.

The Bible teaches us that we have all sinned. What is sin? sin, according to the Bible, is anything we do that does not live up to God's perfect standard. This is not to say that God is a hateful being, unwilling to accept anyone who is not as good as Him. Consider this; in my house, I set certain standards for how people are to be treated and how anyone in my house is going to behave. Anyone who is not willing to meet those expectations simply isn't allowed in my house. I don't hate them, they just can't be here if they're going to violate the boundaries that my wife and I have set up. With God, that standard is perfection.

If we are honest, we would have to admit that none of us have lived a perfect life. This is where the good news comes in. You see, Jesus did live a perfect life. Then He gave his life on the cross to pay the price for our sins. But, He didn't just die on the cross. He rose from the dead and is alive today.

Because of what Jesus did, we can all be forgiven of our sins, no matter how big or small we may think they are.

The Bible says that if you confess with your mouth that Jesus is Lord, and believe that God raised Him from the dead, we can be saved. This seems simple enough. What it's telling us is that if we say that Jesus is the Lord of our lives. In other words, if we are willing to live our lives for Jesus and not for ourselves, then we can be saved.

So, what now?

There is no specific prayer or ritual you have to do to be saved. Still, many people find it helpful to say a prayer. There is nothing magic about these words that you pray. What I always recommend is simply that you tell God how you feel. Tell him about your sin. Not necessarily every sin you've ever committed, but just recognize that you have sinned. Then ask God to forgive you. Lastly, celebrate that you have been forgiven.

If you'd like to talk with someone about this, feel free to email me at matt@restoringnurses.com

Chapter Twelve

Appendix B – The Restored Life Assessment

As I've mentioned previously in this book, the first step towards starting any journey is recognizing where you are starting. I designed this assessment to help you identify that starting point. This assessment does not assess your performance in these different areas. You already know that I do not claim to be an expert in these areas. If you want an assessment of your physical health, see your doctor or a trainer. If you want an assessment of your mental health seek out a qualified mental health professional. This assessment is designed to assess your habits in each of the 6 Pillars of the Restored Life. These habits, I believe, will move you towards that restored life you deserve.

The assessment

Take out a sheet of paper, and number it 1-6. As you read through the assessment, write down your score for each question next to the appropriate number for that pillar. When you are done, add up the total scores for each section. The section with the lowest score represents the pillar where your habits might be the least healthy. This may or may not be the pillar that FEELS the most urgent for you. I would wager that, in most cases, if one of the pillars is in an emergency state then the habits are likely lacking in that area.

If you'd prefer to download a free copy of the assessment that you print and fill out, you can do so at restoringnurses.com/assessment.

The Restored Life Assessment for Nurses

Pillar 1: Work Health

1. On average how many weeks per month do you work more than 40 hours?

   a. Every week (1 point)

   b. 3 weeks (2 points)

   c. 2 weeks (3 points)

   d. 1 week (4 points)

   e. Rarely (5 points)

2. In the past 3 months, how many times have you missed personal/family events because of work?

   a. More than 10 (1 point)

   b. 7-10 (2 points)

   c. 4-7 (3 points)

   d. 1-3 (4 points)

   e. 0 (5 points)

3. On average what percentage of your vacation time do you use each year?

   a. Haven't had a vacation in years (1 point)

   b. I use a little bit of it (2 points)

   c. Probably around half (3 points)

   d. I use most of it (4 points)

   e. I pretty much use it all (5 points)

4. On average, how often do you think about work, while not at work?

   a. Feels like I'm constantly thinking about it (1 point)

   b. 2-3 times per day (2 points)

   c. Daily (3 points)

   d. 1-2 times per week (4 points)

e. Rarely (5 points)

5. I find my current job to be fulfilling

    a. Strongly disagree (1 point)

    b. Disagree (2 points)

    c. Neutral (3 points)

    d. Agree (4 Points)

    e. Strongly agree (5 points)

6. My work environment is physically and mentally safe

    ○ Strongly disagree (1 point)

    ○ Disagree (2 points)

    ○ Neutral (3 points)

    ○ Agree (4 Points)

    ○ Strongly agree (5 points)

Pillar 2: Physical Health

1. How much moderate activity (exercise) do you get per week?

    a. 30-60 minutes (2 points)

    b. 60-90 minutes (3 points)

    c. 90-150 minutes (4 points)

d. More than 150 minutes (5 Points)

e. Less than 30 minutes (1 point)

2. How much water do you drink per day?

a. Does coffee count (I never drink water) (1 point)

b. Very little (1-2 bottles) (2 points)

c. I try to get 3-4 bottles (3 points)

d. At least a gallon per day (4 points)

e. Usually about half my body weight in ounces of water (5 points)

f. Does coffee count (I never drink water) (1 point)

3. How many days per week would you say you eat 3 or more servings of vegetables?

a. Maybe one day (2 points)

b. 2-3 days (3 points)

c. 4-5 days (4 points)

d. Almost every day (5 points)

e. What's a vegetable? (Never or almost never) (1 point)

4. On average, how many nights, per week do you get 7- hours of sleep?

a. Almost never (1 point)

b. 3 (2 points)

c. 4 (3 points)

d. 5 (4 points)

e. Pretty much Every night (5 points)

5. How many sugary drinks do you drink per day (soda, sweet tea, etc.)

a. More than 6 (1 point)

b. 5-6 (2 points)

c. 3-4 (3 points)

d. 1-2 (4 points)

e. None (5 points)

6. How much screen time do you get per day? (Does not include time at a computer for work)

a. It's always on (1 point)

b. More than 5 hours (2 points)

c. 4-5 hours (3 points)

d. 2-3 hours (4 points)

e. Less than 2 hours (5 points)

Pillar 3: Mental Health

1. On average, how many nights, per week do you get 7- hours of sleep?

    a. Almost never (1 point)

    b. 3 (2 points)

    c. 4 (3 points)

    d. 5 (4 points)

    e. Pretty much Every night (5 points)

2. On average, how much time do you spend on social media per day?

    a. More than 3 hours (1 point)

    b. 2-3 hours (2 points)

    c. 1-2 hours (3 points)

    d. Less than 1 hour (4 points)

    e. Almost none (5 points)

3. On average how many times per month do you take time to just rest?

    a. None (1 point)

    b. Maybe once a month (2 points)

    c. A couple of times a month (3 points)

    d. Probably 3 times per month (4 points)

e. Every week (5 points)

4. On average how many times per week do you spend time outside?

    a. I hate the outside (1 point)

    b. 1-2 times per week (2 points)

    c. 3-4 times per week (3 points)

    d. 5-6 times per week (4 points)

    e. Every day (5 points)

5. Outside of work, how often do you connect with other people?

    a. Rarely (1 point)

    b. 1-2 times per week (2 points)

    c. 3-4 times per week (3 points)

    d. 5-6 times per week (4 points)

    e. Every day (5 points)

    f. How often, on average, do you do journaling of any sort? (gratitude, prayer, or regular journaling of events and feelings)

        i. I really have never journaled (1 point)

        ii. Only when I'm in a difficult time (2 points)

      iii. 2-4 times per month (3 points)

      iv. 2-4 times per week (4 points)

      v. Every day (5 points)

Pillar 4: Spiritual Health

1. On average, how often do you spend time with your faith community or people with similar beliefs and values?

      a. Seldom (1 point)

      b. A few times a year (2 points)

      c. Once a month (3 points)

      d. 2-3 times per month (4 points)

      e. Weekly (5 points)

2. On average, how often do you take part in some sort of service to others (outside of work)?

      a. Seldom (1 point)

      b. 1-2 times per year (2 points)

      c. 3-6 times per year (3 points)

      d. About once a month (4 points)

      e. Pretty much every week (5 points)

3. On average, how often do you donate money to your church

or other charitable organization?

   a. Never (1 point)

   b. 1-2 times per year (2 points)

   c. 3-6 times per year (3 points)

   d. About once a month (4 points)

   e. Pretty much every time I get paid (5 points)

4. On average, how often do you read/study your Bible?

   a. Never (1 point)

   b. When I think about it, but not very often (2 points)

   c. 2-3 times per month (3 points)

   d. 1-3 times per week (4 points)

   e. 4 times per week or more (5 points)

5. On average, how often do you intentionally practice gratitude?

   a. I don't really think about it (1 point)

   b. Only when it comes to my mind (2 points)

   c. Maybe once a week (3 points)

   d. 2-4 times per week (4 points)

   e. Daily (5 points)

6. On average, how often do you pray?

    a. Only when something bad happens (1 point)

    b. Occasionally (2 points)

    c. 2-4 times per week (3 points)

    d. 5-6 times per week (4 points)

    e. Daily (5 points)

Pillar 5: Relational Health

1. How many meals, per week, do you eat as a family, at the table?

    a. 0 (1 point)

    b. 1 (2 point)

    c. 2-3 (3 points)

    d. 4-5 (4 points)

    e. 6 or more (5 points)

2. How many times, per month, do you intentionally set aside time to spend with your spouse/partner?

    a. 0 (1 point)

    b. 1 (2 points)

    c. 2 (3 points)

d. 3 (4 points)

e. 4 or more (5 points)

3. How many times, per month, do you intentionally set aside time to spend with your child/children (if you don't have kids score this as a 5)

    a. 0 (1 point)

    b. 1 (2 points)

    c. 2 (3 points)

    d. 3 (4 points)

    e. 4 or more (5 points)

4. On average how often do you spend time with friends, with or without your spouse/partner?

    a. What are friends (1 point)

    b. 2-4 times per year (2 points)

    c. Every couple of months (3 points)

    d. About once a month (4 points)

    e. 2 or more times per month (5 points)

5. On average, how often do you express gratitude to your spouse/partner, children, friends, or other family members?

    a. When I think about it (1 point)

b. 2-3 times per month (2 points)

c. Weekly (3 points)

d. 2-3 times per week (4 points)

e. Daily (5 points)

6. On average, how often do you intentionally spend time away from your spouse/partner and kids? (work doesn't count)

a. Almost never (1 point)

b. Maybe 2-3 times per year (2 points)

c. Monthly (3 points)

d. 2-3 times per month (4 points)

e. Weekly (5 points)

Pillar 6: Financial Health

1. If you lost your income today, how long could you cover basic expenses?

a. I don't even know (1 point)

b. Less than 1 week (2 points)

c. 1-3 weeks (3 points)

d. 1-2 months (4 points)

e. 3-6 months (5 points)

2. Not including your mortgage, how much debt do you have?

   a. More than $100,000 (1 point)

   b. $50,000 - $100,000 (2 points)

   c. $20,000 - $50,000 (3 points)

   d. Less than $20,000 (4 points)

   e. Zero (5 points)

3. How comfortable are you with your current plan for retirement?

   a. I don't think I'll ever be able to retire (1 point)

   b. I may not have to work full-time, but it may be pretty close (2 points)

   c. I will probably still have to work a little when I retire (3 points)

   d. It may be tight, but I should be able to retire when the time comes (4 points)

   e. I'm confident that I'll be able to retire comfortably when the time comes (5 points)

4. If you died today, would your family be taken care of financially?

   a. I don't like to think about that (1 point)

   b. We've talked about it, but haven't done anything (2

points)

   c. I have a little life insurance, but not enough (3 points)

   d. I have adequate life insurance, but no will (4 points)

   e. I have adequate life insurance and a will (5 points)

5. How would you describe your budgeting habits?

   a. I don't write a budget or track my spending (1 point)

   b. I track my spending (2 points)

   c. I have a budget that I look at from time to time, but seldom update it (3 points)

   d. I budget each month and track my spending a couple of times a month (4 points)

   e. I write a budget and track my spending at least once per week. (5 points)

6. In the past 12 months, how often have you been concerned about your ability to pay your bills?

   a. It's a struggle every month (1 point)

   b. 6-8 out of 12 months (2 points)

   c. 2-5 out of 12 months (3 points)

   d. 1-2 out of 12 months (4 points)

   e. Never (5 points)